"The authors run the 'five types of theology' (cf. Frei, Dulles) analytic on the subject of biblical theology and helpfully describe and evaluate—with many a sharp insight—models that range from James Barr to Francis Watson. Issues of whether biblical theology is descriptive, thematic, chronologically ordered, kerygmatic, christological, or trinitarian (or all of these in some combination) are never far from the discussion in a pithy text that never gets distracted from the task. A flame that leapt up in St. Andrews has now a hearth in Los Angeles!"

—*Mark W. Elliott, Senior Lecturer in Church History and Postgraduate Director, School of Divinity, University of St. Andrews*

"A number of scholars have from time to time declared the demise of biblical theology; yet it turns out to be alive and well, or at least to be the continuing subject of lively discussion. *Understanding Biblical Theology* is a useful map of the field. It presents a helpful typology of approaches and is clearly written. It will provide readers with much help in finding their way around this disorienting landscape."

—*John Goldingay, David Allan Hubbard Professor of Old Testament, Fuller Theological Seminary*

"Klink and Lockett have performed a much-needed service—first, by identifying major issues in contemporary study of biblical theology; second, by demonstrating the variety of ways that scholars have tackled these issues; and third, by introducing and assessing key contributors to the conversation. The result is a point of entry into the whole discussion that is as accessible as it is valuable."

—*Joel B. Green, Professor of New Testament Interpretation, Fuller Theological Seminary.*

"Biblical Theology—scholars and pastors alike drop the phrase effortlessly, but no one's quite sure what it really means. And in recent years the misunderstanding and frustrations have only multiplied. Now here comes *Understanding Biblical Theology*, a primer for the uninitiated and a map for the theologically well-versed. If there is any hope for biblical theologians to stop talking past one another, it's time we had a conversation about the conversation. A book like this is just the place to start."

—*Nicholas Perrin, Franklin S. Dyrness Chair of Biblical Studies, Wheaton College Graduate School*

"The popularity of biblical theology shows no signs of abating, but the variety of approaches to the subject can be confusing and daunting. Klink and Lockett provide a landscape for understanding the discipline by setting forth five different approaches to biblical theology. The much-needed work fills a large gap and will be received gratefully by both professors and students."
— *Thomas R. Schreiner, James Buchanan Harrison Professor of New Testament Interpretation, The Southern Baptist Theological Seminary*

"This much-needed book goes a long way toward sorting out the different enterprises that go by the name 'biblical theology' and clarifying the key issues. The authors are competent cartographers whose map of the contested terrain — a spectrum of five positions, each of which occupies a particular position with regard to polar 'north' (i.e., theology) and 'south' (i.e., history) — will prove invaluable to future students. The authors wisely choose to include chapters featuring closer examinations of leading proponents of each theory, neatly sidestepping the temptation to construct straw types. *Understanding Biblical Theology* is a ground-breaking work in the true sense of the term insofar as it calls for those in the academy and church alike to give renewed attention to, and to make serious attempt to say, what it means for biblical theology to be biblical (and theological!)."
— *Kevin J. Vanhoozer, Research Professor of Systematic Theology, Trinity Evangelical Divinity School*

A Comparison of Theory and Practice

UNDERSTANDING
BIBLICAL
THEOLOGY

EDWARD W. KLINK III

DARIAN R. LOCKETT

ZONDERVAN

ZONDERVAN.com/
AUTHORTRACKER
follow your favorite authors

To our wives: Laura Klink and Nicole Lockett

ZONDERVAN

Understanding Biblical Theology
Copyright © 2012 by Edward W. Klink III and Darian R. Lockett

This title is also available as a Zondervan ebook.
Visit www.zondervan.com/ebooks.

Requests for information should be addressed to:

Zondervan, *Grand Rapids, Michigan 49530*

Library of Congress Cataloging-in-Publication Data

Klink, Edward W., III.
    Understanding biblical theology : a comparison of theory and practice / Edward W. Klink III
    and Darian R. Lockett.
        p. cm.
    Includes index.
    ISBN 978-0-310-49223-8 (pbk.)
    1. Bible — Theology. 2. Bible — Hermeneutics. I. Lockett, Darian R. II. Title.
BS543.K63 2012
230'.041 — dc23   2012014668

Cover design: Christopher Tobias
Cover photography: Photoservice Electa / GettyImages
Interior design: Matthew Van Zomeren

Printed in the United States of America

HB 05.09.2024

CONTENTS

Part 4
TYPE 4: BIBLICAL THEOLOGY AS CANONICAL APPROACH

Part 5
TYPE 5: BIBLICAL THEOLOGY AS THEOLOGICAL CONSTRUCTION

Conclusion
UNDERSTANDING BIBLICAL THEOLOGY

ACKNOWLEDGMENTS

This book is the result of a decade-long wrestling with the nature and practice of biblical theology, beginning in St. Andrews, Scotland, and moving to La Mirada, California. Our own foray into the complexity of biblical theology was greatly facilitated by the Scripture and Theology seminar that we participated in at St. Mary's College, University of St. Andrews, from 2002–2005, while we were both doctoral students. The seminar was directed by Professor Christopher Seitz, who with the help of several other faculty members created one of the most deeply engaging learning environments of our academic careers. Foisted upon us was the intersecting dialectic of not only biblical studies and theology, but also the church and the academy. It was in that seminar room that biblical theology became both the problem and the promise of our academic and ministerial work. We would like to extend our gratitude to Professor Seitz and the Scripture and Theology group for the contribution made to us and to this book.

This book has also been forged in light of our present academic setting, Talbot School of Theology, Biola University, where we both spend much time teaching on or around biblical theology. We are privileged to serve at such a wonderful institution and are well aware that it is only because of the amazing ethos of Talbot/Biola that we were able to find the time, resources, and encouragement to write this book. Both of us received Research and Development Grants from Biola University, which provided essential space for research and writing. Thanks are also due to the deans of Talbot, Dennis Dirks and Mike Wilkins, as well as to our colleagues at Talbot, especially Jon Lunde, Ken Berding, Matt Williams, Doug Huffman, Joanne Jung, Jeff Volkmer, Clint Arnold, Uche Anizor, Matt Jenson and Ken Way, for the intellectual and personal support and guidance they have provided us.

We would also like to thank Zondervan, especially our editor, Katya Covrett, not only for the guidance she gave to the project as a whole, but also for her keen insights along the way. Her vision for the place of this volume in Zondervan's larger project on biblical theology gave us confidence to address such a complex topic.

Thanks are also due to Kevin Vanhoozer, who looked at an earlier draft of our project and offered helpful insights and personal encouragement. We are also thankful for the careful read given to an earlier draft of the book by two sections of Klink's upper-level class on biblical theology in the undergraduate biblical and theological studies department at Biola University during the spring semester 2012. The opportunity to see how the book helped them make connections in their understanding of the Bible and its theology gave us the motivation we needed to complete the book. Susan Moeller offered a careful reading of the text for style and expression significantly improving the clarity of the work. Finally, we were helped with many important details by Jason Smith, a graduate student at Talbot and teaching/research assistant of Klink, whose assistance not only made this book better, but also offers clear insight into his own skill as a biblical theologian. Special thanks to Jason Smith and Ryan MacDonald for compiling the indices.

There have been two people, however, who have been standing behind this book long before our decade-long wrestling with biblical theology even began. While they never attended the Scripture and Theology seminar in St. Andrews, they had to listen to hours of our ramblings along the way. Without reading one word of the book, they have offered more guidance and support to it than everyone mentioned above. During each step of the way they have each continued to function as the mothers of each of our three children and as our best friends. This book is dedicated to our wives: Laura Klink and Nicole Lockett.

ABBREVIATIONS

OT Old Testament
PTR *Princeton Theological Review*
SBET *Scottish Bulletin of Evangelical Theology*
SHS Scripture and Hermeneutics Series
SJT *Scottish Journal of Theology*
ST Systematic Theology
STI Studies in Theological Interpretation
SVTQ *St. Vladimir's Theological Quarterly*
TynBul *Tyndale Bulletin*
WTJ *Westminster Theological Journal*

INTRODUCTION: A SPECTRUM OF BIBLICAL THEOLOGY

Is the Bible for the church or the academy, for the people of faith or the scholars of ancient history? Should we read the Bible as the Word of God for the church or as an artifact of history? Ironically, *biblical theology* has been used for all of these divergent perspectives and agendas. *Biblical theology* has become a catchphrase, a wax nose that can mean anything from the historical-critical method applied to the Bible to a theological interpretation of Scripture that in practice appears to leave history out of the equation altogether.

We suspect that on the ears of many the term *biblical theology* might seem more obvious than it is in actuality. Is not "biblical theology" a theology that is characterized by the Bible (thus, a "theology" described by the attendant adjective)? Viewed in this light, biblical theology is a "theology that accords with the Bible, scriptural theology."[1] While intuitively correct, the problem with this definition is evident—all forms of Christian theology claim to be based in some way on the Bible.[2] Whether neoorthodox theology or evangelical theology, from Paul Tillich to Wayne Grudem, each theologian will declare that their theology is seeking to understand biblical revelation. We might say that Wayne Grudem's theology is "biblical" in comparison to Paul Tillich's theology, but both in their own way are seeking to understand the Bible and thus articulate a biblical theology.

---

1. Gerhard Ebeling, *Word and Faith* (trans. James W. Leitch; Philadelphia: Fortress, 1963), 79.
2. For a helpful exploration in this regard see David H. Kelsey, *Proving Doctrine: The Uses of Scripture in Modern Theology* (Harrisburg, PA: Trinity International, 1999).

A second, and widely accepted, understanding of biblical theology is "the theology contained in the Bible, the theology of the Bible itself."[3] Rather than describing a modern work of theology as either "biblical" or something else, here "biblical theology" is the theology contained within the Bible. Within this understanding of biblical theology is the implicit distinction between the theology of the Bible itself—the Bible's own theology—and the way that theology is to be understood and applied today. In other words, this view recognizes a distinction between a *descriptive* biblical theology and a *prescriptive* biblical theology; that is, a historical description of what the Bible teaches is theologically distinct from, yet related to, the ongoing theological teaching of the Bible to be lived and applied in the contemporary world. Even those who accept that the Bible is divinely inspired and normative for faith will acknowledge that the Bible still has to be interpreted and applied in each new generation. This second way of understanding "biblical theology" is a relatively modern development and has significantly affected all modern reflection on biblical theology.

A VERY BRIEF HISTORY[4]

Most discussions of biblical theology begin with a reference to the famous inaugural address given by J. P. Gabler at the University of Altdorf in 1787 entitled "An Oration on the Proper Distinction between Biblical and Dogmatic Theology and the Specific Objectives of Each."[5] Though not the first to use the term *biblical theology*,[6] Gabler argued for the strict separation of biblical theology and church teaching (dogmatics). Rather than allowing traditional church teaching to control the formulation of biblical theology, Gabler

---

3. Ebeling, *Word and Faith*, 79.
4. This brief history of biblical theology can be supplemented with the following texts: Brevard S. Childs, *Biblical Theology of the Old and New Testaments: Theological Reflections on the Christian Bible* (Minneapolis: Fortress, 1992), 1–25; Charles H. H. Scobie, *The Ways of Our God: An Approach to Biblical Theology* (Grand Rapids: Eerdmans, 2003), 9–29; and James K. Mead, *Biblical Theology: Issues, Methods, and Themes* (Louisville: Westminster John Knox, 2007), 1–58.
5. The Latin title reads: "*Oratio de justo discrimine theologiae biblicae et dogmaticae regundisque recte utriusque finibus.*" See J. Sandys-Wunsch and L. Eldredge, "J. P. Gabler and the Distinction between Biblical and Dogmatic Theology: Translation, Commentary, and Discussion of His Originality," *SJT* 33 (1980): 133–58. Gabler is important not because he was the first to advocate separating biblical theology from dogmatic (churchly) theology, but because in this brief speech he gave such clear and concise articulation to an idea that had been percolating in the Enlightenment atmosphere for some time.
6. "Contrary to those who consider Gabler's oft-quoted address on biblical and dogmatic theology as the origin of an 'independent biblical theology,' Scobie points to Simon, Spinoza and Semler as the true pioneers of such an approach" (Karl Möller, "The Nature and Genre of Biblical Theology," in *Out of Egypt: Biblical Theology and Biblical Interpretation* [ed. Craig Bartholomew et al.; SHS 5; Grand Rapids: Zondervan, 2004], 42–43).

argued that biblical theology should be a historical concept—that is, that it should proceed from historical argument. Thus biblical theology could and should be pursued quite independently from the church's dogmatic biases. By means of this strongly rationalist approach, Gabler's historically driven notion of biblical theology was primarily descriptive in nature.

Significant for Gabler was a critical judgment against a necessary connection between the religion of the OT and that of the NT. Committed to a developmental understanding of religion, a guiding premise for Gabler was the notion that religious convictions and practices develop and change through time. Therefore through diachronic historical reconstruction (a kind of "excavation" process), he argued that biblical theology was merely an independent historical project, which could proceed without reference to larger synthetic questions (especially those of the dogmatic teachings of the church). The effect is that roughly from the time of Gabler up until the twentieth century, biblical theology and systematic theology were viewed in sharp contrast with one another.

The largely intractable relationship between systematic (dogmatic) and biblical theology inherited by the heirs of Gabler remained in place especially in the academy.[7] Yet, with his inaugural address as the first Professor of Biblical Theology at Princeton Theological Seminary in 1892, Geerhardus Vos explicitly argued for the reunion between these long separated brothers.[8] Unfortunately, Vos's concerns have too often been ignored by scholars; yet, as we will see, his insights have proved foundational for understanding biblical theology. Whereas there is a pervasive contemporary assumption propagated by many, especially conservative interpreters, that biblical theology is closer to the text of Scripture, Vos articulates his view that the familial resemblance between systematic and biblical theology is that of siblings, not parent-to-child.

> There is no difference in that one would be more closely bound to the Scriptures than the other. In this they are wholly alike. Nor does the difference lie in this that the one transforms the biblical material, whereas the other would leave it unmodified. Both equally make the truth deposited in the Bible undergo a transformation: but the difference arises from the fact that the principle by which the transformation is effected differs in each case. In Biblical Theology this principle is one of historical, in Systematic Theology it

---

7. While the terms "dogmatic," doctrinal," and "systematic" are used as descriptions for theology— throughout this text we will use these terms interchangeably to refer to what is now recognized as the academic subdiscipline of systematic theology.
8. Geerhardus Vos, "The Idea of Biblical Theology as a Science and as a Theological Discipline," in *Redemptive History and Biblical Interpretation: The Shorter Writings of Geerhardus Vos* (Phillipsburg, PA: Presbyterian and Reformed, 2001), 23.

is one of logical construction. Biblical Theology draws a *line* of development. Systematic Theology draws a *circle*.[9]

In other words, biblical and systematic theology equally construct their individual projects by abstracting data from the biblical texts. It is not as if biblical theology is somehow closer to what the text actually says and systematic theology further through philosophical abstraction. Rather, Vos argues that the disciplines are parallel, noting correctly that they both must abstract from the text; where systematic theology relies heavily on logic (or philosophy) as an abstracting aid, biblical theology relies heavily on history as an equally abstracting agent. Thus the two disciplines are siblings, both participating in abstraction in order to reach understanding. For Vos, again in our estimation correctly, both kinds of abstraction are necessary for a theological understanding of Scripture.

Some might reply that biblical theology rests closer to the text because it uses history in its approach to the text. The reason for this assumption is that the Bible is historical and, like history, moves forward to God's ultimate purpose. However, this response assumes that history, as a discipline, is free from methodological concerns, a tenet not all types of biblical theology uphold. That is to say, some types of biblical theology are not comfortable defining history as a given, neutral set of facts that one need only discover and from which one can draw conclusions. History looks much like a "plain" reading of the Bible because both history and a narrative plotline move forward in time. Yet, history is more than just a forward-moving sequence of connected events. History assumes that the direction of development moves in only one direction, forward in time (only diachronic, not synchronic). History also assumes that the most important truth-conveying quality of a text is its ability to refer to "what really happened" (namely, to the event in history). As we will see, reducing biblical theology to mere events in history has led to a dead end.

Shortly after the Second World War and in response to certain European influences, a Biblical Theology Movement emerged, primarily in America. Its goal was to accept biblical criticism without reservation while recovering a robust, confessional theology. While the Biblical Theology Movement was in no way monolithic, it exhibited several general characteristics: (1) the rediscovery of the theological dimension of the Bible; (2) the unity of the whole Bible; and (3) the revelation of God in history.

Unfortunately, according to Langdon Gilkey, a main opponent of the Biblical Theology Movement, the problem with biblical theology was that it was

---

9. Geerhardus Vos, *Biblical Theology* (Grand Rapids: Eerdmans, 1948), 24–25 (emphasis original).

"half liberal and modern, on the one hand, and half biblical and orthodox on the other, i.e., its world view or cosmology is modern, while its theological language is biblical and orthodox."[10] The movement's language, though straightforwardly God-centered, was contained as a whole "within gigantic parentheses marked 'human religion.'"[11] Such a position could only hold together for a short while until the two different cosmologies became unraveled. While the death of the Biblical Theology Movement did not kill biblical theology, it did, like throwing water on a grease fire, spread its elements in all sorts of different directions.

A NEXUS OF ISSUES

Now, from the time of Gabler—for the last 225 years—there has been a bewildering number of ways "biblical theology" has been pursued, giving rise to a host of "problems" that need to be addressed.

Old Testament Connection to New Testament

For at least the last two hundred years, the modern discipline of biblical theology has been divided into the distinct subdisciplines of Old and New Testament theology. Because of the vastly different historical and social contexts of the OT and NT, modern critical study has strengthened the radical distinction between these two bodies of literature. Yet the relationship between the OT and NT stands as one, if not the, central issue in a "whole Bible" biblical theology. For example, Craig Bartholomew argues, "Utterly central to biblical theology must be the question of the Old Testament–New Testament relationship, and this needs to be carefully nuanced."[12] Any truly biblical theology must address how to relate the OT and NT without forcing either out of shape. Brevard Childs, someone who has devoted much of his life to biblical theology, claimed that the relationship of the two Testaments is "the heart of the problem of Biblical Theology."[13] One could add the voice of Christopher Seitz to this list. His work has consistently drawn attention both to the relationship between the two Testaments as well as the particular issue of how the OT exerts a pressure of its own, rather than merely being heard as the NT receives it.[14]

---

10. Landgon Gilkey, "Cosmology, Ontology, and the Travail of Biblical Language," *JR* 41 (1961): 194–205 (194).
11. Ibid., 197.
12. Craig Bartholomew, "Biblical Theology and Biblical Interpretation: Introduction," in *Out of Egypt*, 11.
13. Childs, *Biblical Theology of the Old and New Testaments*, 78.
14. For his most recent and comprehensive statement, see Christopher R. Seitz, *The Character of Christian Scripture: The Significance of a Two-Testament Bible* (STI; Grand Rapids: Baker, 2011).

If the interconnection between the Old and New Testaments stands as the central issue for biblical theology, one's understanding of *how* they relate together becomes important. Though here we will only introduce the complexity of biblical theology, with special emphasis on the various issues involved in approaching biblical theology, it is helpful to list briefly the way some scholars have suggested connecting the Old and New Testaments: prophecy and fulfillment; christological readings; thematic connections (which would include NT use of the OT in quotations); salvation history; and canonical context. As one can imagine, these various proposals of relating Old and New Testaments serve to create the various types of biblical theology we will explore below.

Historical Diversity versus Theological Unity

Standing alongside the question of the relationship between the Testaments is how one should understand the content of Scripture. That is, should readers of the Bible stress the diversity or unity of the Bible's content? On the one hand, taking into account all the various perspectives, contexts, and literary genres contained in the Bible inevitably leads to stressing the Bible's diversity. Matthew's story about Jesus is quite different from John's, or the kinds of holiness at issue in Leviticus are quite different from those in Paul. This would surely be a faithful reading in that one attends to what is actually there. Flying at such a low-level allows the reader to discern the distinct contours of biblical typography and to gain careful and detailed perspective of each discrete text. Yet, the consequence is the proverbial moment of missing the forest for the bark on one tree.

On the other hand, readers could stress the overarching unity of the Bible. This kind of reading engages specific passages of the text with the question of how it all fits together always in mind. Any one passage or book must be understood as a part of the biblical story line. In the attempt to discern the theological unity of the biblical material, some have proposed a central theme (note the connection to the issue of the OT's relationship with the NT), which holds the diversity of perspectives and contexts together under one umbrella idea. It is precisely here that biblical theology has been implicated in the "unity-diversity debate." Karl Möller notes: "Biblical theology has been found guilty of reducing or obscuring the diversity of the biblical material in its quest for the Bible's unity."[15] Yet the very DNA of biblical theology requires representing the biblical material in a unified form — so much so that some dismiss biblical theology as forcing orderliness when the Bible itself lacks such order.

---

15. Möller, "The Nature and Genre of Biblical Theology," 56.

Scope and Sources of Biblical Theology

The relation between the Testaments and the nature of their unity (or diversity) raises the question of the scope of biblical theology: What am I looking for? The questions of the relationship between the OT and NT and between unity and diversity press us toward this question. Is the scope limited to the original authors and readers of Scripture, or can it also include the contemporary readers? And if it is limited to the historical past, a question still remains, which one? For some, biblical theology is so confined to the theology of the Bible in its original historical situation that the theology of the Pentateuch, for example, cannot transcend itself so as to network with later theologies within the Bible (e.g., the Minor Prophets). But if it is limited to the historical past, how can the Bible still be claimed to have a contemporary theological status and authority?

The scope of biblical theology controls the nature of its sources, which asks the question: Where am I going to find what I am looking for? The closer the scope of biblical theology resides in the original social and historical context of the Bible, the more necessary is the use of extrabiblical sources, in order to develop an understanding of the issues and context "behind the text." However, where the canon is preferred — that is, a biblical theology that is more intratextual in nature — there is less warrant for a search beyond (or without) the actual biblical text itself. While it is common for scholars to agree on the use of sources outside of the biblical canon, there is disagreement regarding the status and function of extrabiblical sources in discerning the theological message of the Bible.

Subject Matter of Biblical Theology

The question about scope and sources has at its foundation the question of the context for reading Scripture, which finds support among the already mentioned nexus of issues (e.g., church vs. academy). These issues press forward toward the goal of biblical theology, or the thing to which the theology of the Bible points. The search for the subject matter of biblical theology is rooted in the following question: About what or whom does biblical theology speak?

The options for the subject matter of the Bible are as diversified as the people who suggest them. Is history the subject matter, or God, or the actions of God, or the belief of the writers? Even more, how is the subject matter to be constructed from the Bible? According to Mead, the debate over the legitimate subject matter of biblical theology is reaching a consensus among scholars, at least as it centers on an important distinction between the content of the biblical writings and the content of the biblical writers.[16] This distinction finds itself at the end of the progressing nexus of issues of biblical theology. What one assumes about the relation between the OT and NT, diversity and unity, and the scope and sources of biblical theology goes a long way toward giving definition to its subject matter.

Biblical Theology as a Churchly or Academic Discipline

A final question that cuts through the discussion of biblical theology is whether its task is that of the church or the academy. Should pastors and church leaders be expected to "do" biblical theology as they preach, teach, and pastor individuals in the church? Or, is biblical theology a discipline with such a degree of complexity and nuance that it must be left to the professional scholar?

Much of this question depends on who may claim the rights to a religious "text." By asking whether biblical theology is a task for the church or the academy, one must consider whether biblical theology is prescriptive or descriptive. If it is prescriptive — that is, the theology of the Bible must be understood as both speaking to our modern world and authoritative for Christian life and practice — then one would assume that the church must necessarily be committed to biblical theology. A key component of discipleship and evangelism should include an understanding of how the biblical story reveals the one, coherent will of God for the world today.

However, if biblical theology is descriptive — namely, only the historical task of outlining what ancient peoples believed about their God — it would only be of antiquarian interest and thus fail to be central to the modern church's task. Of course one can see the implications. If biblical theology is merely descriptive, the pastor would have little time for it, and it would likely only be of interest to the historian; but if biblical theology is prescriptive, church leaders would properly take it up as a churchly task. The implications of each position goes a long way in defining the sources of biblical theology.

THE BOOK ITSELF

Understanding Biblical Theology attempts to define "biblical theology" by describing various theories and practices of contemporary biblical theology. Using a spectrum balanced on either end by history and theology, five types of biblical theology are plotted between these poles, as more or less "theological" or "historical" in concern and practice. As each type is discussed, we will necessarily address each of the perennial issues raised above: the relationship

---

16. Mead, *Biblical Theology*, 244.

between the OT and NT; the *historical* diversity and the *theological* unity of the Bible; the scope of biblical theology and whether the sources should be restricted to the Christian canon or broadened to include noncanonical sources; the subject matter of biblical theology; and finally, whether biblical theology is a task for the church or for the academy. Though offered as only a heuristic schema, placing each type on the spectrum in relationship to each other provides readers with a starting point for understanding and assessing the theory and practice of biblical theology.

Each of the five types finds definition in two separate chapters of the book. For each of the types, one chapter gives the theory of that particular type, followed by a further chapter that gives an example of that approach in practice by describing the work of a modern "biblical theologian" who exemplifies that type of "biblical theology." Although there is minimal dialogue between the types, except for the brief assessment of each modern biblical theologian, the parallel positions of the five types between the frames of the introduction and conclusion offer the reader numerous venues for assessment and synthesis among the various theories and practices of biblical theology.

The plotline for identifying each of the types spans the continuum from history to theology. These two, though interrelated, constitute the terminal points on the spectrum. Each approach is concerned in varying degrees with both history and theology, but the plotline clearly demonstrates whether the type leans more heavily toward history or theology as a *primary* means of retrieval. When this judgment can be made, it is instructive to note how, for example, an imbalance toward history might restrict the concern for theology and vice versa. Again, we must note that (1) this is a heuristic construct developed for the purpose of learning, and (2) we as the authors of this book have made judgments throughout as to what point on the line any one individual interpreter belongs. This plotline is, therefore, merely a simplified cartograph; it is not intended to be a definitive account of biblical theology. In our view, even if a reader may want to adjust the position of one of the types (or their modern examples), the construct presents a successful tool.

The Types

Finally, we should give an outline of the types themselves. This guide map will be helpful to keep in mind as the types are discussed in further detail. The survey of the five types move from more historical (type 1) to more theological (type 5). A chart offering a simplified summary for comparison is provided in the conclusion. In fact, after reading the introduction we recommend reading the chart in the conclusion before turning to the main text.

We envision this chart as a kind of topographical map alerting readers of elevations and depressions as they navigate the main text

HISTORY..THEOLOGY

Type 1	Type 2	Type 3	Type 4	Type 5
Historical Description	History of Redemption	Worldview-Story	Canonical Approach	Theological Construction

Type 1: Biblical Theology as Historical Description

The first type is the most historical because it is strongly framed by the category of history and the task of the historian. BT1 is entirely descriptive; concern for present-day religion and meaning is intentionally kept out of sight. While theologians are concerned with "what it means," BT1 is only concerned with "what it meant." This approach to biblical theology desires to free itself from the anachronistic interpretations of its predecessors and to force itself to accept the hiatus between the time and ideas of the Bible and the time and ideas of the modern world. Thus, BT1 makes certain that history—the specific biblical history—is the sole, mediating category. The biblical "theology" is the theology believed by the people back then, the theology of the Bible as it existed within the time, languages, and cultures of the Bible itself; it is a purely historical and descriptive discipline.

For this reason there can be no whole-Bible theology since the theology of the different authors, let alone the different Testaments, is hardly uniform or unified. To connect the OT with the NT is to do a disservice to them both, for while the NT belongs to Christians, the OT can only belong to the Jews. Only this way can the theology of the Bible be "in its own terms." BT1 is dependent, therefore, on contemporary research done entirely by the academy (not the church), is in no way bound to the so-called biblical "canon," and is primarily an exegetical task (discovering what the text meant). The "theology" of the confessing church, in the opinion of BT1, has already moved beyond the Bible by translating its theology into its own social-historical context.

Type 2: Biblical Theology as History of Redemption

The second type is also strongly historical and is similarly framed by history and the task of the historian, but its primary category is redemptive history. One step removed from BT1, BT2 is concerned to establish a whole-Bible theology, but similar to BT1, BT2 demands that the whole-Bible connections be made with historical resources. What holds the Bible together is still history, but a "special history" that is derived by theological criteria. The Bible reveals a History of Redemption progressing in a chronological manner. The history of redemption is visible through tracing the major themes and overarching structural ideas (e.g., covenant, kingdom, and promise and fulfillment) as they develop along a sequential and historical timeline. The biblical "theology" is only accessible through the lens of God's (historical) progressive revelation.

In this way biblical theology is theological primarily in the manner it defines and utilizes history and is supported by the various themes running through the biblical narrative that serve as the connecting fibers between the biblical parts, including the OT and NT. While the historical nature of BT2 is directly parallel to the work of the academy, the goal is a biblical theology for the church. For this reason BT2 is a strongly exegetical task with an eye to God's unfolding purposes throughout the ages. Such a bifocal hermeneutic tends to bend between a "what it meant/what it means" hermeneutic of Scripture. This interconnected approach to biblical theology has developed into different strands rooted in different ecclesial and academic traditions.

Type 3: Biblical Theology as Worldview-Story

The third type represents the middle of the spectrum, a notoriously difficult position to nail down, and it is strongly framed by the category of narrative, which is both a literary and philosophical category. In an attempt to balance historical and theological concerns, BT3 discerns the overarching "story shape" or narrative connection between the OT and NT as constitutive of the Bible's "theology." Read as a continuous and interconnected narrative, this approach discerns the narrative continuity running throughout the whole Bible. Many working with this narrative structure of the Bible's unity would not consider this approach as biblical theology per se; rather, the concerns that shape this type of reading originate from a desire to read Scripture without historical criticism functioning as the primary methodology. Like BT2, the interconnectedness of this approach lends itself to several different trajectories; yet at its center is the category of narrative, which seeks to balance literary, historical, and theological elements in Scripture.

As a middle position, BT3 does not begin with front-loaded theological propositions or purely descriptive historical reconstruction, yet it uses a measure of both history and theology—under the larger category of narrative—to assist the construction of the biblical worldview-story. While its historical approach to the biblical narrative is directly parallel to the work of the academy, the guidance provided by the resources of theology has much to commend it to the church. The complexity of BT3, like any story, has numerous versions. But this approach to biblical theology offers a thick, intertextual reading of the whole Bible that serves to coalesce the diverse parts of the Bible with the whole, as well as the story of God with the story of its readers.

Type 4: Biblical Theology as Canonical Approach

The fourth type is strongly framed by the category of canon, which is both a historical and theological category. Working hard to articulate a perspective on the relationship between biblical studies and theology, "canon" for BT4 serves to enjoin the historical meaning of the ancient text with the contemporary meaning of Christian Scripture. A canonical interpretation of Scripture assumes some operational convictions regarding the identity, character, and literary sources of revelation or truth. While a canonical approach is difficult to define and is variously applied, what is uniform is the focus on the canon's ability to reflect the diverse uses and applications of Scripture.

The canon is a path that has been traversed by many travelers, each of whom has left many footprints. The final form of the canon, therefore, is a collection of tradition "handlings," with the final form being the last shaping of the tradition. In this way the canon preserves a collection of "tradition shapings," which maintain fidelity to the original material and simultaneously promote the adaptation of the material for a new setting and situation. For this reason the canon itself becomes the overarching context for handling history and theology and for determining the meaning of the Bible. Such an approach allows the biblical "theology" to be both descriptive and prescriptive. Similar to BT3, BT4 contains elements of both academy and church: the academy is needed to explore the textual traditions that have been received, collected, transmitted, and shaped throughout different times, cultures, and languages; the confessing church is needed as the applied audience for whom the texts serve as their life for identity and obedience. Ultimately the canon establishes Scripture as a witness that presents the Bible's true subject matter: the gospel of Jesus Christ.

Type 5: Biblical Theology as Theological Construction

The fifth type is strongly framed by the category of theology as it is defined and used by the confessing church. After presenting a critique of the abuses of historical criticism, BT5 positions itself within the confines of the confessing church. BT5 is associated with a growing interest in a theological interpretation of Scripture, which intentionally positions itself outside the academy's "departmentalization" of biblical studies and systematic theology with its bifurcation between ancient text and contemporary Scripture. This leads to the conviction that the Bible properly belongs to the church, and that for Christians the Bible is *their* Bible, not the Bible of foreign people in a foreign time and land. For this reason the task of biblical theology is an integrated exegetical-hermeneutical discipline with overriding theological concerns, incorporating biblical scholarship into the larger enterprise of Christian theology.

Such a starting point demands that the only home for such a method is the church, not the academy. BT5 must incorporate and be ruled (e.g., the Rule of Faith) by faith commitments, that is, theological presuppositions. This is no public discussion, for biblical theology is the sole practice of the church, the confessing community. This is not to say that such a use of biblical theology is uncritical, but only to claim that the concern is not with secular models of truth, but with in-house models defined entirely by the confessing church. While this approach has a variety of nuances, the central tenet is that it requires a theological hermeneutic that leads to the formation of a "theological construct," allowing the Bible to function as God's Word for the church.

CONCLUSION

In the end, *Understanding Biblical Theology* offers a fivefold taxonomy of how biblical theology is currently defined and practiced in an effort to offer substance and clarity concerning the elusive idea of biblical theology. Though offered as only a heuristic schema, placing each type on the spectrum in relationship to each other provides readers with a starting point for understanding and assessing the theory and practice of "biblical theology." This book is not an answer to the problem of defining biblical theology; rather, it is the initiation of a dialogue that hopes to clarify the notion of biblical theology and to encourage its practice in the life of both the academy and the church.

We have written this book primarily because we wanted to read it! Our own journey through the morass of biblical theology convinced us several years ago that more definition of theory and practice was needed. This book is the result of our own desire for understanding biblical theology, not only because it is its own subdiscipline in the academy, but also because it plays such an important role in the church. We hope you are as enthusiastic at the prospect of reading this book as we have been over the opportunity to write it.

Part I

TYPE 1: BIBLICAL THEOLOGY AS HISTORICAL DESCRIPTION

Chapter I

BIBLICAL THEOLOGY AS HISTORICAL DESCRIPTION: DEFINITION

The first type of biblical theology (BT1) has many similarities to the influential History of Religions School[1] in the nineteenth and early twentieth century, in which a new picture emerged of the people, ideas, and institutions of the ancient world. This new picture resulted in a purely descriptive study of the Bible. The most important advocate for making the descriptive approach a dominant type of biblical theology is Krister Stendahl. In 1962, Stendahl provided what has become a definitive statement of what we are calling BT1.[2] According to him, this new picture of the Bible was rooted in a growing empathy for the Bible's own patterns of thought:

> It became a scholarly ideal to creep out of one's Western and twentieth-century skin and identify oneself with the feelings and thought patterns of the past. The distance between biblical times and modern times was stressed, and the difference between biblical thought and systematic theology became much more than that of diversification over against systematization or of concrete exemplification over against abstract propositions. What emerged was a descriptive study of biblical thought.[3]

---

1. The History of Religions School is the name given to a group of Protestant scholars in Germany over a century ago who intended to understand the OT and NT as religion(s) within the context of their historical environments, including a comparison with other religions of that time and region. Cf. Richard N. Soulen, *Handbook of Biblical Criticism* (2nd ed.; Atlanta: John Knox, 1981), 167–68.
2. Krister Stendahl, "Biblical Theology, Contemporary," in *IDB*, 1:418–32.
3. Ibid., 418.

Stendahl calls this new phenomenon a "mature outgrowth of the histori-cal and critical study of the Scriptures."[4] The descriptive approach waived—or intentionally kept out of sight—any concern for present-day religion and faith. The History of Religions School had emphasized the widening of the gap "between our time and the time of the Bible, between West and East, between the questions self-evidently raised in modern minds and those presupposed, raised, and answered in the Scriptures."[5] Thus, Stendahl, employing a method similar to a History of Religions approach, explicated this divide between two poles—past and present—with the following qualifying methodological ques-tions: "What *did* it mean?" and "What *does* it mean?" (Or more simply, "what it meant" and "what it means"). The former, "what it meant," is alone the task of biblical theology; "what it means" is the task of dogmatics (systematic theology).

The key difference between BT1 and other theological approaches was the question of relevance for today. Neither "liberals" nor "conservatives" had allowed for a gap between the times, for both were methodologically ignorant of the contemporary limitations of the Bible's content. Both were convinced that the Bible contained revelation that was in the form of eternal truth, with little concern for the Bible's historical limitations. The disagreement between liberals and conservatives up to that point concerned the *results* of translating revelation, not whether such a translation was historically possible or appro-priate. It was BT1, and its definitive presentation by Stendahl, that desired to free itself from the anachronistic interpretations of its predecessors, and to force itself to accept the hiatus between the time and ideas of the Bible and the time and ideas of the modern world.

Thus, BT1 made certain that history—the specific biblical history—is the sole, mediating category. We are entitling BT1 "Biblical Theology as Historical Description," since its method is entirely controlled by a historical-critical methodology that is descriptive in nature.

THE TASK OF BIBLICAL THEOLOGY

What is most certain for BT1 is that biblical theology is *not* the same as doctrinal (systematic) theology. This distinction is important and must be maintained. The reason this is important is because for most "the very idea of 'biblical theology' seems to hang uncertainly in the middle air, somewhere between actual exegesis and systematic theology."[6] This middle position has

---

4. Ibid.
5. Ibid., 419.
6. James Barr, *The Concept of Biblical Theology: An Old Testament Perspective* (London: SCM, 1999), 3.

often allowed it to be a sort of hybrid—part exegetical and part theological—and even more, has allowed biblical theology to be utilized and claimed by both sides. Hence, most proponents of BT1 quickly separate their biblical theology from a more doctrinal or confessional biblical theology. Stated succinctly, *the task of BT1 is to affirm the exegetical or descriptive nature of biblical theology and deny the theological or normative nature of biblical theology.* This can be supported by several necessary explanations.

First, biblical theology is the theology of the Bible as it existed within the time, languages, and cultures of the Bible itself. It is the theology of the Bible "in its own terms."[7] Biblical theology is past-tense theology, not present-tense or contemporary theology. But even if we speak of a biblical "theology," we speak not of a universal theology, or what Stendahl called a "normative" theology,[8] but a theology that has a specific social location: the Bible's social location. That is, we speak of the theology of the Bible as the religion of the Bible's earliest recipients.

BT1, therefore, is entirely controlled by a context far removed from the present context; it is looking not for a theology for today, but for the theology that existed back there and then. Truth statements (or normative judgments) from theology are left for the systematic theologian of contemporary Christianity (religion). Since we are looking for a biblical theology that existed in the context of ancient minds regarding an ancient text, the task of biblical theology can usually be done only by biblical scholars—and almost always is. Even more, because the task is necessarily attentive to original social locations, a further division is commonly created between the two Testaments, or the two Bibles, one Hebrew and one Christian. It is for this reason that most proponents of BT1 reject a two-Testament biblical theology. There can be no pan-biblical theology simply because the "pan" obliterates two very different social-historical-religious contexts.

Second, biblical theology is something new in the sense that it is the result of contemporary research methods. Biblical theology is not, therefore, something already laid down in a past or ancient tradition—the creeds or confessions of the church. "The theology of the Bible, as most modern biblical scholarship has envisaged it, is something that *has still to be discovered.*"[9] The biblical theologian is not rehearsing what is already known, but is exploring what can be found. Its foundation and its mode of scholarly identification are different in kind from the foundation and mode of scholarly identification of any one of the traditional theological positions or parties.

---

7. This is the oft-stated phrase of Stendahl, "Biblical Theology, Contemporary," 430.
8. Krister Stendahl, "Method in the Study of Biblical Theology," in *The Bible in Modern Scholarship* (ed. J. Philip Hyatt; Nashville: Abingdon, 1965), 196–209.
9. Barr, *Concept*, 3.

In a sense, biblical theology transcends the traditional theologies, not merely between different theological parties and denominations within Protestant Christianity, but also between Protestant and Catholic theologies, even Christian and Jewish theologies. A true theology of the Bible — a true biblical theology — is not confined to one tradition, but absorbs them all without bias or limited foundation. In the end, it becomes a uniting force, a stabilizer, not a proponent of one of the competing traditions. The reason for this is that it does not work from the end of the religious trajectory (today, with all of its different parties), but from the beginning (the past, from the womb of the religion itself). Since BT1 is purely descriptive, it is always working at more accurate descriptions of the theology of the Hebrews or Christians, and it is benefited by each new discovery and each new theory that explains what is unclear or unknown. It is the antithesis of the creed or confession.

Third, biblical theology is an exegetical project. Stated another way, according to BT1 advocates, biblical theology is something that is done by biblical scholars, not by theologians. By holding firmly to the exegetical nature of biblical theology, BT1 makes the determinative factor of its definition the question of historical criticism.[10] John J. Collins explains it this way:

> Whether or not one can conceive of a biblical theology grounded in historical criticism obviously depends on whether one insists on a faith commitment that exempts some positions from criticism, or whether one is willing to regard biblical theology as an extension of the critical enterprise that deals with truth-claims and values in open-ended engagements with the text.[11]

It is the latter definition of biblical theology that BT1 endorses: a biblical theology that is grounded in historical criticism in such a way that faith commitments are off the table, and a biblical theology that is an extension of the critical enterprise. For this reason some avoid altogether calling the enterprise "biblical theology." John Barton, for example, though adopting the same descriptive method as Stendahl, does not refer to the theology of the Bible as "biblical theology." As Barton explains, "I would rather characterize the kind of theology that is associated with biblical criticism [his alternative title for historical criticism] as *critical theology*."[12] By "critical," Barton helpfully guides the understanding of BT1 as a task rooted in the historical-critical

---

10. Robert Morgan, "New Testament Theology," in *Biblical Theology: Problems and Perspectives: In Honor of J. Christiaan Beker* (ed. Steven J. Kraftchick, Charles D. Myers Jr., and Ben C. Ollenburger (Nashville: Abingdon, 1995), 105, considers it fortunate "for the integrity of the discipline" that most NT theologians are trained in historical criticism.

11. John J. Collins, *Encounters with Biblical Theology* (Minneapolis: Fortress, 2005), 3.

12. John Barton, *The Nature of Biblical Criticism* (Louisville: Westminster John Knox Press, 2007),

method and controlled by the historical-critical agenda. Once one leaves a "critical theology," they have left the first part of a two-part process. And the two parts are "what it meant" and "what it means." As Barton explains:

> Assimilating any text, the Bible included, is a two-stage operation. The first stage is a perception of the text's meaning; the second, an evaluation of that meaning in relation to what one already believes to be the case. This process cannot be collapsed into a single process, in which meaning is perceived and evaluated at one and the same time and by the same operation.[13]

BT1 is not dealing with truth, the determination of contemporary meaning, but with text, the determination of ancient meaning. While the former is the task of the theologian, the latter is the task of the historian. The truth question is (and can only be) asked once the text has been critically analyzed; and the results of the truth question are unimportant to the task of the first-order historical critic. For, according to proponents of BT1, the task of biblical theology is to be descriptive, not prescriptive.

THE USE OF BIBLICAL THEOLOGY

If the task of biblical theology for BT1 is historical and critical, the use of biblical theology is the object of the academy, not the church. Biblical theology of this sort cannot be ruled by prior faith commitments, nor can it be laden with creeds and confessions. It must be "a subject for public discussion regardless of faith commitments."[14] Thus it must fit universal standards of objectivity, not limited by religious communities or tainted by religious commitments. Even more, "it is concerned with truth-claims and ethical values presented by the biblical text, and in any critical biblical theology these claims and values are open to question."[15]

While several proponents of BT1 are hesitant to consider a place for biblical theology outside of the academy, there are those who do give some guidelines for its use in the church. For example, according to Stendahl, maintaining a "what it meant/what it means" distinction has "considerable

---

185. For a similar designation see Gerd Theissen, *On Having a Critical Faith* (trans. John Stephen Bowden; London: SCM, 1979).

13. Barton, *Nature of Biblical Criticism*, 159. Stendahl, "Biblical Theology, Contemporary," who institutionalized this two-part process ("meant/means"), actually divides the second part into two halves: interpretive translation and normative relevance. As we will see below, these two halves still function to answer the dogmatic question of "what it means" (for today), which is entirely distinct from the "what it meant" question of biblical theology.

14. Collins, *Encounters with Biblical Theology*, 3.

15. Ibid.

ramifications" for the preacher, "if he in any sense sees it as his task to communicate the message of the Bible to the congregation whose shepherd he is." Such a statement brings sharp focus to the topic of preaching: the message *of the Bible*. Of course, Stendahl is well aware of the difference—the hiatus—between the message of the Bible in its ancient social location and the message(s) of contemporary social locations. Thus, Stendahl compares the preacher's task to that of a translator—a bilingual translator, who is capable of thinking in two languages (not Greek and Hebrew, but the language of both an ancient and modern social location):

> His familiarity with the biblical world and patterns of thought should, through his work in descriptive biblical theology, have reached the point where he is capable of moving around in his Bible with idiomatic ease. His familiarity with the "language" of the contemporary world should reach a similar degree of perception and genuine understanding. Only so could he avoid the rhetorical truisms of much homiletic activity, where the message is expressed in a strange—sometimes even beautiful—mixed tongue, a homiletical Yiddish which cannot be really understood outside the walls of the Christian ghetto.[16]

This vision for preaching is propelled by a concern *for the Bible*. For "a mere repetition and affirmation of the biblical language, or even a translation which mechanically substitutes contemporary terms—often with a psychological slant—for those of the original, has little chance to communicate the true intention of the biblical text."[17] The vision for preaching promoted by BT1 demands, for biblical reasons, that the two contexts be separated. A consistent descriptive approach gives to the church an exposure to the Bible in its original intention (in its own terms), "as an ever new challenge to thought, faith, and response."[18] This is no theology of Augustine, Aquinas, Calvin, or Schleiermacher; rather, it is much more: a true theology of the Bible.

THE SCOPE AND SOURCES OF BIBLICAL THEOLOGY

Since the descriptive task of BT1 demands that the social location of the Bible is the only viable context from which to draw forth the Bible's true theology, the context of the Bible becomes the guide to its scope. The theol-

---

16. Stendahl, "Biblical Theology, Contemporary," 430.
17. Ibid.
18. Ibid., 431.

ogy of BT1 is not determined by the meaning known and implied by the church or by any other period outside of the Bible's own social-historical context. As Barr explains, the "scope is determined by the meanings as known and implied within the time and culture of the Bible."[19] Thus, at the most basic level, the sources of biblical theology are any and all religious materials used by the Hebrew or Christian believers to explain or express their God-religion. This raises two important questions. First, since many of the religious books were used by numerous "faiths," does this mean that BT1 is really the same thing as the History of Religions School? Second, what about the canon, Hebrew or Christian? We will deal with each of these in turn.

Since BT1 applies a rigid descriptive approach to biblical theology, it does have many similarities to the History of Religions School. John H. Collins has admitted that "scholars have often found it hard to distinguish between biblical theology and the history of Israelite religion."[20] The History of Religions School was fueled by the discovery of ancient texts, giving extracanonical insight into biblical religion. This was also a central feature of biblical theology, for it provided new information to assist with the descriptive task: exploration of remoter parts of the world, discoveries of unknown civilizations, the beginnings of anthropology, the decipherment of ancient languages, the discovery of papyri and scrolls, and the reading of inscriptions — things which, unlike the Bible, "had not been handed down through long ages of interpretation but still existed as they had lain for thousands of years."[21]

Thus, as we return to our question — Is BT1 the same as the History of Religions School? — the answer must be negative. Even those like Rainer Albertz and John Barton, who link them so closely together, are not willing

---

19. Barr, *Concept*, 74.
20. John H. Collins, *The Bible after Babel: Historical Criticism in a Post-Modern Age* (Grand Rapids: Eerdmans, 2005), 99. Collins does not think they are indistinguishable. While he does see similarities between Israelite religion and Near Eastern religion, he is convinced that "there seems to have been an exclusivistic strain in Yahwistic religion from very early times, even if it did not always dominate. The point here is not that any particular feature was entirely unique to Israel, but that differences in degree and emphasis give the religion a configuration that becomes quite distinct over time" (128). Cf. Yehezkel Kaufmann, *The Religion of Israel: From Its Beginnings to the Babylonian Exile* (Chicago: Univ. of Chicago Press, 1960), who argues for a sharp distinction between "pagan religion" and "Israelite religion." For a method seeking less distinction, see Patrick D. Miller, *Israelite Religion and Biblical Theology: Collected Essays* (JSOTSup 267; Sheffield: Sheffield Academic, 2000), who unites the History of Religions School and biblical theology by allowing for "the interplay of continuity and discontinuity that is always going on" (376).
21. Barr, *Concept*, 101.

to describe them as synonymous.[22] Though BT1 and the History of Religions School are certainly related in genetics and method, they are not the same thing. The difference is not always easily apparent. Collins states it too simply: "The primary basis for a distinction lies in the weight given to nonbiblical sources in the latter enterprise [History of Religions]."[23] A more nuanced definition is the following: biblical theology emphasizes the intellectual aspects of the religious context—ideas, formulas, arguments, mental concepts, theological developments—all as they can be derived from written texts. History of religions, by contrast, emphasizes cultural aspects of the religious context—customs, rituals, architecture, relation to groups and classes, social, economic, and political setting, and psychology. Barr summarizes these emphases as having a difference in scope and field:

> The one, Old Testament theology, is related to *certain texts* and to the theology *implied* by them; the other, history of religion, is related to a large social and intellectual field, for which these texts are part of the evidence, and often indirectly so, through hints they give of the contemporary world rather than through the values that they directly affirm.[24]

Biblical theology aligns itself with the *message* of a biblical book as communicated by the author. A NT theology, for example, impresses the reader with a theology of John or Paul; it does not present a theology of Judas Iscariot or the Judaizers. The book, not the context, determines the scope. Thus, while the relation between biblical theology and history of religions is one of "overlap and mutual enrichment," because "the stuff of which biblical theology is built is really biblical religion," the two are different.[25] If nothing else, there is a pragmatic difference: "the same material which is historically ordered and described by the historian of religion may perhaps be more topically and thematically organized by the biblical theologian."[26]

---

22. See Rainer Albertz, *A History of Israelite Religion in the Old Testament Period* (2 vols.; trans. John Bowden; Lousiville: Westminster John Knox, 1994), especially the "Introduction"; and John Barton, "The Messiah and Old Testament Theology," in *King and Messiah and the Ancient Near East: Proceedings of the Oxford Old Testament Seminar* (ed. John Day; JSOTSup 270; Sheffield: Sheffield Academic, 1998), 365–79. Albertz even sees the two as, in some way, competing: "If the discipline of 'the history of Israelite religion' has a real chance to develop itself again in the theological faculties, the future will show which of the two competing disciplines is more appropriate to the subject of the Old Testament" (16). Albertz does not disguise his favoring the history of religion "as the more meaningful comprehensive Old Testament discipline," which, interestingly, he argues, "will be better able to assist the transfer of Old Testament research to theology and the church" (16). Such language fits similarly beside Stendahl's vision for preaching already discussed above.
23. Collins, *The Bible after Babel*, 99.
24. Barr, *Concept*, 133.
25. Ibid., 135.
26. Ibid.

We now turn to the second question: What about the canon? The close relation between biblical theology and history of religion makes this clear: the descriptive approach can give no significance to the canon. As Stendahl explains, "The church has a 'Bible,' but the descriptive approach knows it only as the 'Bible of the church.'"[27] Since the theology of BT1 is rooted in the original social location, it is not merely the texts of the Old and New Testaments that are important, but all related texts, even the so-called non-canonical or extracanonical. Their historical location makes them not just important but necessary. A closed or fixed list of books for determining theology is rejected in principle. The argument against canon is not merely principled, for as John Barton has proclaimed:

> But there is no reason to think that the first generation of Christians gave a moment's thought to exactly which books these were. One of the least plausible of all ideas ... is the notion that Jesus and his disciples had hard and fast views on which books ought to be reckoned scriptural. Neither Jesus nor Paul nor anyone else in the early Church, so far as we can tell, had any assumptions about this question.... Like them they mostly took it for granted that the books that were read in the synagogue and quoted by teachers and scholars constituted "the books," as Scripture was sometimes loosely known.[28]

But the central factor that undermines "canon" is that it is not — cannot be — a part of the descriptive task. It is an unhesitatingly prescriptive pronouncement that can have no place in a biblical theology "in its own terms."[29]

THE HERMENEUTICAL APPROACH OF BIBLICAL THEOLOGY

BT1 attempts to determine, as objectively as possible, what sort of "theology" existed in ancient times. The term "objectively" means "independently of whether one advocates this theology or disapproves of it, or thinks it is the

27. Stendahl, "Biblical Theology, Contemporary," 428. See also Stendahl's statement in "Method in the Study of Biblical Theology," 198: "He who says Bible says Church."

28. John Barton, *People of the Book? The Authority of the Bible in Christianity* (Louisville: Westminster John Knox, 1988), 25.

29. Stendahl, "Biblical Theology, Contemporary," 430, argues that talk of canon is implicitly a question regarding the meaning of the Bible in the present, which is explicitly not a part of the descriptive approach. Stendahl even compares the arrival of the descriptive approach to a renewal of the Reformation principle to "return to the original." As Stendahl argues, "such a return to the 'original' — given the circumstances of the time — engenders one of the most spectacular renewals of theology and church life that history has ever seen."

ultimate divine revelation, or thinks it does not matter."[30] The hermeneutics of BT1 is governed in every way by historical parameters. These parameters are not meant to be disciplinary exclusive, but to demand that the interpreter be self-critical. "One of the most basic functions of criticism is to criticize, not the Bible itself, but people's understanding of the Bible. And one aspect of this is by showing that texts do not mean what they have commonly been taken to mean.... [Historical criticism] involves being aware of differences between our usage and the Bible's."[31] The task of translating the original, historical meaning of the Bible to today is not the task of biblical theology; rather, that is the task of systematic theology.

Barr suggests that a helpful analogy for this hermeneutical approach is historical theology. "The majority of works in [historical] theology do not take as their subject-matter simply God, or creation, or faith, but the understanding of these themes, or others, in the work *of past theologians*."[32] BT1, like historical theology, cannot work in isolation from other forms of historical knowledge: political, social, and economic. In spite of historical theology's controlling "historical" element, it is also still a theology. "Historical theology lies fully under the constraints of history and historical method, but it continues to be also a form of theology. It is the re-creation of the theology *which lies behind the texts, which existed in the mind* of Augustine or whomever else."[33] In the same way, BT1 pursues the theology that lies behind the text, theology that existed in the minds of the biblical authors. It is a description of the theology of the Bible in its original context attained by historical-critical means.

The history of biblical theology has revealed that all types of biblical theology depend on the progress of the descriptive element; the place of disagreement centers on the present-day meaning derived from descriptive conclusions. The premise of BT1 is that there is a drastic difference between the first century and contemporary centuries, which demands what Stendahl calls "translation." To ignore the difference between then and now ("what it meant" and "what it means") or to be sloppy in translation is detrimental to the theological task. Stendahl explains regarding the nature of this translation:

> ... the way from this descriptive task to an answer about the meaning in the present cannot be given in the same breath on an *ad hoc* basis. It presupposes an extensive and intensive competence in the field of hermeneutics. With the original in hand, and after due clarification of the hermeneutical

---

30. Barr, *Concept*, 196.
31. Barton, *The Nature of Biblical Criticism*, 102–3.
32. Barr, *Concept*, 209.
33. Ibid., 210–11 (emphasis added).

principles involved, we may proceed toward tentative answers to the question of the meaning here and now. But where these three stages [descriptive — translation — normative] become intermingled, there is little hope for the Bible to exert the maximum of influence on theology, church life, and culture.[34]

Stendahl's own hermeneutic is a living example of carefully appropriating these different stages. When confronted with the role of women in the church, Stendahl was convinced that the NT does not allow for women's ordination. Reading the NT in its context and with a descriptive approach made it certain. But this had no bearing, for Stendahl, on the same issue for the present day. Numerous factors have changed the social setting since the NT era; simply to repeat the NT's judgment in modern times would be a mistake.[35] Just as it would be wrong to apply a modern understanding of the role of woman back onto the Bible, it would be wrong to apply a biblical understanding of the role of women onto the modern understanding. Biblical theology is descriptive and historical (stage one) — this is "what it meant." The move to interpretation (stage two) for contemporary, normative relevance (stage three) — "what it means" — is an entirely separate matter and involves other, more primary factors than historical description.

THE SUBJECT MATTER OF BIBLICAL THEOLOGY

The descriptive approach is unable to move beyond the historical context — and historical meaning — of the documents themselves; therefore, the theology of the Bible can only be derived from the original, historical, social location of the Bible. For the biblical theologian, the subject matter is entirely dependent on the *Sitz im Leben* ("life situation") of the documents themselves. Such an approach demands that later theological concepts are not to be imposed anachronistically upon the biblical texts (i.e., theology from the contemporary church, or any period outside of the original social location). The biblical-theological topics find no ground in BT1 for present-day meaning. Rather, meaning for the present requires the two further stages: translation followed by a calculation of what may be normative, and the normative is determined by factors necessarily beyond the historical.

---

34. Stendahl, "Biblical Theology, Contemporary," 422.
35. See, e.g., Krister Stendahl, *The Bible and the Role of Women: A Case Study in Hermeneutics* (trans. Emilie T. Sander; Philadelphia: Fortress, 1966).

Stendahl provides a helpful comparative analysis of the subject matters derived from other methods to biblical theology. Karl Barth, for example, finds an overtly theological subject matter in the Bible. A concentration on an atemporal subject matter—God, Jesus (the Christ), grace, and so on—bridges the gap between the centuries and necessitates their sameness. "This identity in the subject matter guarantees the meaningfulness of the Pauline writings ... since God, Christ, and all of revelation stand above history."[36] Thus, for Barth, the historical tension between then and now is relieved in a theological category of "otherness."

Rudolf Bultmann, a second example, finds an overtly philosophical subject matter. For Bultmann the subject matter is self-understanding, which allows the Bible to be given an anthropological interpretation. "When the NT kerygma witnesses to historical events (as in 1 Cor. 15:3–8), these 'events' are of little significance as events; what counts is to re-create their effect on man's self-understanding."[37]

Oscar Cullmann, a third example, finds an overtly historical subject matter rooted in a specific definition of "time." Though Cullmann does not provide as explicit a hermeneutic as Barth or Bultmann, Stendahl argues that Cullmann's approach is "a religious philosophy of history," which remains even after its translation into the present.[38] But none of these approaches do justice to the true subject matter of the Bible, at least according to BT1.

The subject matter of Barth, Bultmann, and Cullmann are antithetical to BT1 and its descriptive method. Stendahl accuses the above approaches to biblical theology of being "subjectively convinced that they were objective scholars who stated only 'facts.' "[39] The subject cannot be a theological "otherness," or a philosophical self-understanding, or a religious philosophy of history; rather, it must be the subject matter of the texts themselves. The subject matter cannot be atemporal; it can only be historical. The above approaches are completely unchecked, especially once they move from description into their atemporal translation.

In sharp contrast, a descriptive approach provides its own checks and balances. "Once we confine ourselves to the task of descriptive biblical theology as a field in its own right, the material itself gives us means to check whether our interpretation is correct or not."[40] For the concern of BT1 is not present day but

---

36. Stendahl, "Biblical Theology, Contemporary," 422.
37. Ibid., 421.
38. Ibid.
39. Ibid., 422
40. Ibid.

ancient: "our only concern is to find out what these words meant when uttered or written by the prophet, the priest, the evangelist, or the apostle—and regardless of their meaning in later stages or religious history, our own included."[41]

The logic of the subject matter of BT1 is that it is not merely rooted in *the* biblical context, but in any contexts in which the Bible existed—all the "life situations" settled into biblical record. This means that the theology of later biblical texts is not to be imposed on earlier biblical texts. This is more clear with the two Testaments; the former is to be regarded as the Bible for Jews, the latter as the Bible for the earliest Christians. But even within the OT there are different "layers" that need to be described individually. Since the OT contains material from many centuries of Israelite life, the descriptive task is constantly concerned with the "layers of meaning" derived from the history and transmission of OT traditions.[42] For this reason, any descriptive statement about what an OT passage meant "has to be accompanied by an address: for whom and at what stage of Israelite religion or Jewish history?"[43]

The subject matter, therefore, is not mysteriously found outside the biblical text and its context, for enough layers of subject matter lie before the biblical theologian, who describes with great precision the subject matter of the Bible "in its own terms." It does have an "otherness," but only in that the subject matter is not our theology, or philosophy, or our religious history, but the theology of the Bible itself and the people to whom it was originally intended.

CONCLUSION

The first type of biblical theology, "Biblical Theology as Historical Description," seeks a theology of the Bible in its own terms and based on its own context(s). Rather than being tossed around by contemporary faith-related commitments that make normative judgments for the present day, BT1 remains committed to an authority of the Bible that seeks first and foremost its *own* message. Such a concern is not denying a present-day significance; rather, it is concerned that the "what" the Bible is witnessing should be described first, and biblical scholars should leave translation for today to the church and dogmatic theologians. Anything else has not only left the objective, descriptive task of biblical theology, but has left the Bible itself.

---

41. Ibid.
42. Ibid.
43. Ibid. A similar approach would be used for the New Testament, especially regarding the historical Jesus in the Gospels.

Chapter 2

BIBLICAL THEOLOGY AS HISTORICAL DESCRIPTION: JAMES BARR

James Barr (1924–2006) serves as an apt example of doing biblical theology particularly within the limits of history. Though an OT scholar, Barr's interests and competencies ranged across the fields of linguistics, analytic philosophy, history of religions, and theology. Born in Glasgow, Scotland, and educated at Manchester and Oxford, England, James Barr held academic posts in both the UK (Edinburgh and Oxford) and the US (Princeton and Vanderbilt). Because of his influence and international reputation as an astute biblical scholar, he was awarded no less than ten honorary doctorates from various universities around the world. He passed away in 2006 after an eight-year retirement in Claremont, California.

Throughout his long and successful career Barr maintained concern for biblical theology. His first book, *The Semantics of Biblical Language*, took up the linguistic problems associated with biblical theology as it was being practiced in the early twentieth century. Structured more as a critique than a constructive argument, *Semantics* struck at the root of what was then called the "Biblical Theology Movement." Specifically Barr challenged the weak foundation of this kind of biblical theology by questioning several of the "movement's" linguistic assumptions.

First, he challenged the commonly cited difference between Hebrew and Greek ways of thinking, which in turn expressed rather divergent modes of theological discourse. Here Barr detected an undisciplined Romanticism lurking under the assertion that Hebraic thinking was wild, primitive, and passionate and therefore a means to detect or recover the transcendent.[1]

Second, Barr argued against the assumed connection between the definition and history of a particular Hebrew or Greek word and its theological concept. He famously labeled this inappropriate use of language "illegitimate totality transfer," namely, that a word carries with it all of its possible meanings in each particular context in which it appears.

Finally, he rejected the use of etymologies in arguing for a word's meaning. Quite characteristic of Barr's overall project, *Semantics* is a precise and sustained critique of an entire way of using biblical words in order to discover the theological content of the Bible. With *Semantics* specifically in view, Francis Watson considers Barr "biblical theology's most significant and persistent critic."[2] In fact many, including Watson, argue that Barr single-handedly brought about the demise of the "Biblical Theology Movement."

However, to come to the conclusion that Barr rejected biblical theology wholesale would be far from the mark. Though he launched a full frontal assault on a way of doing biblical theology that, in his view, did not take language seriously, Barr maintained a long and sustained interest in theology and the Bible. In the final book of his long career, *The Concept of Biblical Theology* (1999), Barr both summarized the practice of biblical theology throughout the early twentieth century and offered the fullest expression of his own approach to the subject.

DEFINING THE TASK: BARR'S OVERARCHING PROJECT

One of Barr's pervasive concerns was to resist the twin threats of Romanticism and Fundamentalism. For Barr, the Romantic tendencies of the "Biblical Theology Movement" were exhibited in the desire to recover the transcendent through focusing on the Hebraic way of thinking. He was also concerned about

---

1. James Barr, *Semantics of Biblical Language* (London: Oxford Univ. Press, 1961), 8–20; specifically on the issue of "illegitimate totality transfer," see 218, 222. See also similar arguments in Barr's *Biblical Words for Time* (London: SCM, 1962). Moisés Silva notes in general that "Barr's book, *The Semantics of Biblical Language*, was a trumpet blast against the monstrous regiment of shoddy linguistics" (*Biblical Words and Their Meaning: An Introduction to Lexical Semantics* [Grand Rapids: Zondervan, 1994], 18; see also Silva's interaction with Barr throughout).

2. Francis Watson, *Text and Truth: Redefining Biblical Theology* (London: T&T Clark, 1997), 18. Brevard Childs also refers to Barr's criticism of the "Biblical Theology Movement" as "a final blow" (*Biblical Theology in Crisis* [Philadelphia: Westminster, 1970], 65). For this same assessment, see Craig G. Bartholomew, "Biblical Theology," in *DTIB*, 84–90.

Fundamentalism's persistent rejection of historical criticism. Reading the Bible as a direct connection to God's will and authority was unsatisfactory for Barr, who believed the Bible to be primarily a book of history. Barr found the fundamentalist approach to reading the Bible for a normative theology lacking in professionalism.[3] According to Barr, both biblical scholars venturing into theology and theologians dabbling in exegesis were working outside their professional competencies. Theology, like exegesis, should be left to those trained in the discipline. This general characterization of Barr's work is in keeping with his argument that if biblical theology is to be practiced, it must be done on the basis of a rigorously defined methodology and executed by professional historians.

The starting point of any clear methodology for doing biblical theology must, for Barr, begin with definition. If there was to be any attempt at biblical theology, Barr argued that it should be defined as a descriptive task, and this description must primarily be within the confines of history. Barr argued that the "term 'biblical theology' has clarity only when it is understood to mean theology as it existed or was thought or believed within the time, languages, and cultures of the Bible itself. . . . What we are looking for is a 'theology' that existed back there and then."[4]

Furthermore, Barr maintained that biblical theology is something still to be discovered. Biblical theology is not connected to or reliant on previous theological systems, certainly not something handed down by any particular theological tradition. Rather than something directly relevant to the modern world, biblical theology is an historical discipline, which seeks primarily to describe how the Bible communicates what ancient peoples believed and how these beliefs shaped conduct.

However, because biblical theology is often practiced in close relation to the church and modern faith communities, Barr identifies, in his estimation, an internal tension of biblical theology: Is it purely descriptive, or is it also prescriptive? In other words, is biblical theology an historical discipline, which only describes what ancient peoples believed and did, or, in addition to this, does biblical theology also articulate some kind of normative faith and practice for the modern church? Barr formulated this tension as follows: "Does [biblical theology] not only tell us what the theology of biblical times was and explain to us its inner relations and connections as the people of the Bible understood them, but also explain how that theology is to be interpreted and realized in the actual life and thought of the religious community today?"[5]

---

3. See especially Barr's *Beyond Fundamentalism* (Philadelphia: Westminster, 1984), 110–27.
4. Barr, *Concept*, 4.
5. Ibid., 15.

In order to understand Barr's answer to this question accurately, we must first consider whether the Bible actually contains any theology at all, and if so, what kind of theology. For Barr, theology is "a reflective activity in which the content of religious expressions is to some extent abstracted, contemplated, subjected to reflection and discussion, and deliberately reformulated." Here Barr distinguishes between religious opinions or aspirations that do find articulation in the biblical text and the more intentional moment of reflection and sustained discussion of systematic theology. Therefore, he concludes that "much of the Bible does not have this [systematic theological] character."[6] According to these criteria the Bible does not contain much (if any) explicit theology; yet this conclusion does not deter Barr from discerning a theology of the Bible. "One way of expressing the task of biblical theology, or of theological exegesis, is to say that it seeks to make explicit the implicit theology of the texts. But this is needed precisely *because the texts themselves for the most part are not theology.*"[7]

Because, in this technical sense, the Bible does not *contain* theology — or Barr argues we should at least not think of the Bible as *being* theology — the biblical theologian must then focus his investigation on the thought world and culture that lies behind the text. It is there, in the real world of ancient events and ideas, that the biblical theologian will discover realities that exist before or "under" the actual biblical text of which biblical theology is primarily concerned. Thus, biblical theology consists more in "the nature of exegesis rather than that of theology in the proper sense."[8] Again, this discussion of whether the Bible actually is or contains theology is consistent with Barr's emphasis that biblical theology is a descriptive and historical task — a project excavating what ancient people did and believed.

Returning to the question above, it should be clear that though Barr talked of a tension between biblical theology as either descriptive or prescriptive, he considered the discipline to be a descriptive task. This direction in Barr's thought is further evidenced by his hermeneutical method. Following Krister Stendahl's classic formulation,[9] Barr adopted the temporal distinction (though critical of its particular wording) between the historical meaning ("what it meant") and modern significance ("what it means") of biblical texts. Barr insisted that biblical theology is a "descriptive undertaking which, historically, and as objectively as possible, tells us what sort of 'theology' existed

---

6. Ibid., 249.
7. Ibid., 248 (emphasis added).
8. Ibid.
9. See above comments on Stendahl, "Biblical Theology, Contemporary" (p. 33, note 13).

in ancient times."[10] Whether a modern interpreter approves or disapproves of that "theology" is beside the point for biblical theology, because, for Barr, biblical theology is purely a descriptive/historical discipline.

If there is any normative theology articulated in the Bible, it is up to dogmatic theologians to discern; but for Barr, they must make such discernment from the raw data generated by the descriptive and objective discipline of biblical theology. Barr goes on to argue that when the dogmatic theologian takes up the raw data of biblical theology in this kind of normative or prescriptive theological reflection, the theologian also necessarily takes up other relevant (and, again for Barr, necessary) elements such as theological traditions, philosophy, modern social situations, and (most likely) natural theology alongside of biblical theology.[11] It is precisely because of the presence of these other elements that biblical theology does not (and cannot) include modern, prescriptive/normative judgments. As a descriptive, academic task, such theologically normative judgments are beyond the reach of BT1.

CONTINUITY AND THE PROBLEM OF THE CONNECTION BETWEEN THE TESTAMENTS

As a descriptive/historical discipline, Barr articulates a lingering tension within biblical theology. But rather than a tension between the descriptive and prescriptive function of biblical theology (as above), Barr is concerned with the tension between the OT and NT. If biblical theology is concerned with the raw data of historical exegesis — recovering what ancient peoples believed — there is a difficulty in understanding how or even if the OT and NT are related. Does not the OT describe what one particular group of people believed about their God (namely, the Jews) and the NT another (Christians)? Based on a historical description of the content of the Old and New Testaments, each corpus is concerned with rather distinct events (monarchy and exodus vs. resurrection) and main characters (YHWH vs. Jesus).

Highlighting this tension, Barr points to a number of OT theologies that do not include the NT as an integral part of their work. Barr concludes that because such OT theologies have managed to handle accurately the content of OT theology without reference to the NT, this necessarily "points towards the intrinsic separateness of the two fields." He continues, "I suggest that this should be accepted, rather than that vast amounts of further energy be poured

---

10. Barr, *Concept*, 196.
11. Ibid., 202.

into a task that has proved to be neither necessary nor salutary."[12] The task Barr has in mind is the misdirected attempt to construct a theological account of both the Old and New Testaments either by structure or common themes.

Making a related point, Barr notes those OT theologians who maintain that the NT must play a central role in an accurate account of OT theology have actually failed to engage with the NT at all in their work. For example, OT theologies produced by Walther Eichrodt, T. C. Vriezen, and Gerhard von Rad,[13] while insisting on a necessary connection to the NT in practice, fail to engage with the NT or provide evidence of its theological relevance for OT theology. This failure actually proves Barr's point—even those who claim that the NT is necessary for a full account of OT theology fail to demonstrate this connection.

Barr notes that whereas both OT and NT contain implicit theology— which can be articulated in discrete OT and NT theologies—the "theology of the Old Testament is not the same as the theology of the New. When taken as wholes ... they are not congruent, nor even closely analogical."[14] However, to conclude that Barr sees no profit in articulating the theological relationship between OT and NT is wide of the mark. Barr insists, "I am not suggesting that Old and New Testaments do not belong together theologically: as a Christian I believe that it is essential that they do." Rather, he concludes, "the ultimate establishment of relation between Old and New Testament is a matter of faith; or, in other terms, it lies beyond the abilities of biblical theology and belongs to doctrinal theology."[15] Because biblical theology is purely a descriptive task, it cannot account for anything beyond the historical connections between the Testaments—going beyond this would be, for Barr, to move out of biblical theology into systematic theology.

THE SCOPE AND SOURCES OF BIBLICAL THEOLOGY IN BARR'S WORK

This assessment regarding the connection of Old and New Testaments directly shapes the scope of biblical theology for Barr. Rather than OT or NT

---

12. Ibid., 187.
13. See Walther Eichrodt, *Theology of the Old Testament*, 2 vols. (Philadelphia: Westminster, 1961, 1967); T. C. Vriezen, *An Outline of Old Testament Theology* (Oxford: Blackwell, 1958), who specifically claims that OT theology "is a study of the message of the Old Testament both in itself and in its relation to the New Testament" (148); and Gerhard von Rad, *Old Testament Theology*, 2 vols. (New York: Harper and Row, 1962, 1965). Whereas each of these OT theologies argue for the importance of the NT in a theological account of the OT, every one of them fail, in Barr's estimation, to demonstrate textually any real theological connection between the Testaments.
14. Barr, *Concept*, 186.
15. Ibid., 187.

theologies, or works that take up the entirety of the Old and New Testaments together, he contends that any number of exegetically driven studies would count as doing biblical theology. In accounting for the structural and thematic unity of the whole Bible, many forms of biblical theology attempt to grasp the theology of Old and New Testaments taken as wholes and taken together. Typically this drive to see the whole shifts the emphasis of particular works away from narrower, analytic studies of smaller units of text to the broader synthesis of vast amounts of text. For Barr this is a mistake. He argues:

> To think of biblical theology as essentially a task of synthesis at the level of the great complexes is to talk as if there is no problem in the theological understanding of a paragraph in Ezekiel or in Romans, but a problem only in the bringing together of these disparate materials into one.... It is in fact an illusion to suppose that the move from smaller units to larger constitutes a move from non-theological to more theological modes of understanding.[16]

Barr follows this salutary insight by arguing that biblical theology is actually dependent on analytic studies in the realm of textual criticism, linguistics, form-criticism, historical-criticism, and the like.

Because biblical theology necessarily rests on the foundation of such analytical work, he contends that single-volume studies that contain the theology of OT or NT in their title are not the only studies that are concerned with biblical theology. In other words, it is not only the large-scale, single or multivolume work, or the OT or NT theology that participate in doing biblical theology, but also the various monographs, thematic treatments, philological works, along with individual commentaries, all of which constitute biblical theology. On this account Barr comments, "The question, often posed, of 'methodology' in writing a work on biblical theology is thus a relatively unimportant one. There is no such thing as a 'right' methodology for carrying out such a task."[17] Rather than one correct methodology that produces a work of biblical theology, Barr thinks that all the various means of historically centered biblical study helpfully contribute to and in fact constitute biblical theology.

In this vein Barr concludes that biblical theology is not an

> activity sharply separated from other kinds of study that concerns the Bible. It does not have strict rules to demarcate it from other kinds and levels of biblical study.... Information and scholarship of any kind—historical, linguistic, textual, cultural, comparative—can at any point move into the

---

16. Ibid., 141.
17. Ibid., 59.

position of significance for biblical theology. Anyone who wishes can, of course, refrain from making that transition, and can decide simply to keep out of the area of biblical theology.... But their work remains as work that may potentially be significant in the field of biblical theology.[18]

Whether a monograph taking up an historical event situated behind the text, a detailed lexical study of a word's use throughout the Old Testament, or a technical commentary, all equally contribute to or provide the data for biblical theology. For Barr the critical issue is that "biblical theology or Old Testament theology *is in essence not a book but a level of scholarship.*"[19]

Here one can detect the implicit assumption that historical, linguistic, and textual research done by biblical scholars forms the foundation (raw material) that supports larger constructions of biblical theology. A potential problem with this approach is that upon discovering new historical evidence—such as a fragment of a pot with a Greek word bearing a unique meaning—one necessarily must reassess one's entire theological understanding of the text based on this new historical reality. Though understanding of the text must take account of the ever-changing insights of historical-critical reading, such a volatile foundation is an uneasy fault line on which to build the church. It seems this view holds biblical theology hostage to historical discovery so that history ultimately trumps theology.

Barr's understanding of biblical theology's scope has a knock-on effect on what sources one might use to construct a biblical theology. Because the scope of biblical theology includes a myriad of academic or scholarly studies, the sources for biblical theology are much broader than the Old and New Testaments. Barr takes exception to those, such as Walther Zimmerli and Brevard Childs,[20] who insist that OT or NT theologies must be founded exclusively on the Christian canon. In the case of Zimmerli—who claims the Hebrew-Aramaic canon as the exclusive base of OT theology in his methodology—Barr exposes Zimmerli's consistent appeal to noncanonical texts in order to

---

18. Ibid., 61.
19. Ibid., 59 (emphasis original).
20. Walther Zimmerli (*Old Testament Theology in Outline* [Edinburgh: T&T Clark, 1978]) specifically argues that his "presentation of Old Testament theology is based on the Hebrew-Aramaic canon" (1); yet contrary to this claim see his substantial references to the noncanonical texts 2 Maccabees (35, 236) and Ben Sira (80, 158). Brevard Childs also argues for founding OT theology on the Christian canon (see *Biblical Theology of the Old and New Testaments* [Minneapolis: Fortress, 1992]). But even in Childs's work Barr detects a practical dependence on noncanonical works. Childs admits, "Especially in terms of wisdom literature, one senses the contribution of the larger Christian canon represented in the Apocrypha. It is significant that the most important modern treatise on the theology of wisdom by G. von Rad (*Wisdom in Israel*) should also include an extended treatment of Sirach" (Childs, *Biblical Theology of the Old and New Testaments*, 262).

situate OT theological claims. In effect Zimmerli's claim to an exclusive canon is undermined in practice and thus provides Barr with evidence that biblical theology actually relies on more than a Christian canon for its resources.

This, along with what Barr considers the weak Reformation arguments against the inclusion of the Apocrypha into the Christian canon, is proof that the sources for doing biblical theology are in fact much broader than an exclusive Christian (Protestant) canon. Because, as we have seen, Barr situates biblical theology as a historical/descriptive discipline supported by a variety of scholarly disciplines, he even suggests that material from the Dead Sea Scrolls should be included in a proper biblical theology: "The Dead Sea Scrolls, therefore, must be part of the 'canon' for biblical theology, whether or not they are part of the canon of any religious institution of today."[21]

Underlying such a move is Barr's conclusion that "theology was much more important than the canon."[22] Though provocative to some, Barr is consistent on this point. By insisting that biblical theology is purely a descriptive task, he establishes warrant for expanding the sources of biblical theology to include the Apocrypha and the Dead Sea Scrolls. Rather than founding biblical theology on a particularly Christian canon, Barr argues that "theology is not really built upon the canonical books. It is built upon what was *thought*; its base lies *behind* the canonical books, in the life of ancient Israel."[23] It is for this reason Barr can claim that theology is more important than any particular canon. Theology is a product of reflection on ancient, pretextual events and ideas.

Thus, as Barr has maintained all along, biblical theology is a historical task of describing what ancient peoples believed. Here again the implications should be noted. If biblical theology is both a level of scholarship and draws broadly from ancient Near Eastern documents such as the Dead Sea Scrolls, then biblical theology is necessarily a task for the academy and not the pastor or lay teacher. It is an academic discipline rather than an immediate means of theological reflection for the Christian church.

DOING THE TASK: WHO IS QUALIFIED TO DO BIBLICAL THEOLOGY?

If it is correct to think of such analytical work and such broad sources as constituting the foundation for biblical theology, it is then appropriate to ask who is qualified to produce a biblical theology. Barr bluntly states that biblical

---

21. Barr, *Concept*, 580.
22. Ibid., 581.
23. Ibid., 578 (emphasis original).

theology "is something that is done by biblical scholars.... All the major work in biblical theology has been done by biblical scholars."[24] Here Barr clearly understands a "biblical scholar" as first and foremost a historian, not a theologian. He scolds Childs for suggesting that theologians such as John Calvin and Karl Barth were doing biblical theology "depending as they do on *ad hoc* redefinitions of the terminology."[25] According to Barr, rather than doing biblical theology, Calvin and Barth are excellent examples of theologians dabbling in biblical theology precisely because they are concerned with how the theology of OT or NT times relates to contemporary communities of faith.

Barr contends that any such benefit to contemporary religious communities today must be decided by the individual interpreter; such a move is essentially a function of doctrinal theology and not a part of biblical theology. Thus, if Barr's notion of doing biblical theology excludes Calvin and Barth, it is out of the question for the local pastor or lay teacher. His description of biblical theology excludes all but the professional biblical scholar: "The fact that biblical theology has its identity within the Bible's own times, languages and cultures provides ... that biblical theology is something that has to be done, and is done, by biblical scholars—doubtless with some exceptions."[26] One wonders what kind of exceptions Barr might be referring to if the practitioner of biblical theology must be so professionally acquainted with the Bible's own times, languages, and cultures.

Though acknowledging the use of Scripture and biblical theology in the context of the church, Barr argues that in these settings biblical theology is at its greatest risk. Of exegetes going beyond historical description of the biblical text, Barr warns, "For them to go farther and seek to make regulative theological judgments in the sense of what the reality is, of what should be believed and done, can be done only by the importation of dogmatic arguments."[27] Again, any theological voice escaping the ancient world with a normative message for today is well beyond the limits of biblical theology.

BARR'S TURN TO "STORY" FOR DOING BIBLICAL THEOLOGY

Returning to the question of whether the Bible is or contains theology in any real sense, one must ask what kind of theological reflection does biblical theology exhibit. Within Barr's project one must turn to the category of "story"

---

24. Ibid., 2.
25. Ibid., 3.
26. Ibid., 5.
27. Ibid., 58.

to answer this question. Along with many others,[28] Barr argued for the central category of "story" (or narrative) for both OT exegesis and theology. It is especially interesting to note in the present volume (because we are situating biblical theology between the two poles of history and theology) that Barr thought story was a helpful category for biblical theology because it was both like and unlike history. Like history, narrative unfolds "in a temporal progression and tells a story which is cumulative from the beginning along a temporal scale."[29] But unlike history, story shares in the following characteristics. Story draws attention to the whole rather than only those elements that are available to and verifiable by historical events outside the story itself. Again, unlike history, Barr's "story" category emphasizes the sequence of events in the narrative rather than the process of redaction and composition.

Barr gives the example that according to historical sensibilities, the event that lies at the center of the OT may be the pretextual event of the exodus and thus historically could be understood as the beginning of the OT. However, reading the story-shape of the OT sets the beginning at a different moment, namely, the story sequence begins with creation and runs through the experiences of the patriarchs. Here reading the story-shape of the OT is different from running along historically verifiable events. Two final strengths of story for Barr are specifically that story highlights the central place of divine speech within the narrative along with the characteristic of story to focus on identity—both communal and personal identity.

In distancing his approach from other literary or canonical approaches—in clear distinction from the narrative/philosophical approach of BT3—Barr is quick to note that while it is helpful to attend to the story-shape of the text, one need not uncritically accept the story as it stands. Rather than swallowing the story whole without qualification, the historian can (indeed must) read the narrative as a story only then to assess it via historical criticism. Furthermore, while arguing for the central category of story, Barr works hard

---

28. Barr specifically mentions his own work in *Old and New in Interpretation* (London: SCM, 1966) and "Story and History in Biblical Theology: The Third Nuveen Lecture," *JR* 56 (1976): 1–17, along with Dietrich Ritschl and Hugh O. Jones, *"Story" als Rohmaterial der Theologie* (Theologische Existenz heute 192, Munich: Kaiser Verlag, 1976), and Ingrid Schoberth, *Erinnerung als Praxis des Glaubens* (Munich: Kaiser Verlag, 1992). Though Barr does not mention any connection, there is a certain similarity between Barr's use of "story" and N. T. Wright's appeal to a "worldview-story" in his *New Testament and the People of God* (London: SPCK, 1992), 135. He uses this term to set off story as a comprehensive worldview from the various narratives or stories in the biblical text that express that worldview. We will consider Wright's view of "story" in chapter 6. For a helpful comparison, see Craig G. Bartholomew and Mike W. Goheen, "Story and Biblical Theology," in *Out of Egypt: Biblical Theology and Biblical Interpretation* (ed. Craig Bartholomew et al.; SHS 5; Grand Rapids: Zondervan, 2004), 153–67.

29. Barr, *Concept*, 345.

to distinguish story from theology. Specifically rejecting von Rad's thesis (which suggests that "the most legitimate form of theological talk about God is the rehearsal of narrative"),[30] Barr contends that "story is not theology, but is the 'raw material' of theology.... It may 'be theological' in the sense that it invites theology or calls for it, or requires theological interpretation; but it is not in itself theology. It is raw material for theology."[31]

Though his work is overwhelmingly characterized by a critical stance toward other strategies of doing biblical theology, here Barr comes closest to offering an account of how he might produce a work of biblical theology himself. Attending to the development of events and characters as they unfold within the story is a helpful way of detecting the flow and unity of the Bible. And this emphasis is consistent with the narrative shape of Scripture.[32] But even while offering the constructive category of story as a means of detecting the implicit theology of the text, Barr is careful to redirect attention back to the historical events that lie behind their narration in the story. While forwarding the category of story, Barr remains resolute in his resistance to approaches to biblical theology that privilege the final form of the text as they leave behind both the "pre-textual realities and stimuli" and redactional layers of testimony witnessing to these events. Though finding story a helpful category, Barr's focus remains fixed on the historical events standing behind the text.

ASSESSMENT

In the end for Barr, biblical theology is done by biblical scholars (as opposed to theologians or pastors), seeks something "new" or innovative (e.g., rather than merely restating something handed down from the past—doctrinal theology), is essentially ecumenical, and is firmly set in a particular historical context. His enduring contribution to the field of biblical theology is his unrelenting and blistering critique of the work of others.[33] The strength of his legacy remains one of keeping the discipline honest and insisting that rigorous methodology be applied to one's work.

Nevertheless, this strength also constitutes a major weakness. Only offering a critique of what is wrong in the synthesis of others, Barr fails to describe

---

30. Von Rad, *Old Testament Theology*, 1:121.
31. Barr, *Concept*, 354.
32. See Barr's comments: "Thus in general, although not all parts of the Bible are narrative, the narrative character of the story elements provides a better framework into which the non-narrative parts may be fitted than any framework based on the non-narrative parts into which the story elements could be fitted" (*Concept*, 356).
33. For this judgment see D. Penchansky's article "Barr, James," in *Historical Handbook of Major Biblical Interpreters* (ed. Donald K. McKim; Downers Grove, IL: InterVarsity Press, 1998), 423–27.

how he would go about writing a synthetic work of biblical theology. Furthermore, his definition of biblical theology as a "level of scholarship," while aptly describing Barr's own work, offers no clear method for actually doing biblical theology. Barr's most constructive comments fail to offer guidance forward in the discipline and seem to be slightly self-serving in that his definition of biblical theology fits his own project exactly.

Despite the limited value of his overly critical focus, Barr does insist on several relevant and helpful criteria for doing biblical theology. One seeking to construct a biblical theology should follow Barr in seeking a relative objectivity that is willing to reexamine one's theological convictions and assumptions in light of historical and cultural research. Barr is also correct to draw attention to the significance of work being done in the various fields of biblical studies. Too often insights generated from more analytic or narrow studies are ignored or misunderstood for their contribution to the field of biblical theology. Finally, though clearly overemphasized in Barr's work, we must affirm the necessary role history plays in constructing a biblical theology.

Still, while appreciating Barr's emphasis on history, we are not well served by his reductionistic definition of biblical theology. If it is "a level of study that is present in varying degrees in all sorts of teaching, courses, texts, dictionaries, encyclopedias, articles and books,"[34] how then does one determine what "level of study" constitutes the level of biblical theology? If biblical theology is identified with works of biblical studies of various kinds performed at a particular "scholarly level," then a bewildering degree of work counts as biblical theology. The interests of biblical theology are not best served by allowing it to become a "catch-all" term.

A further critical assessment of Barr is a result of his insistence on historical description as biblical theology. Emphasizing pretextual events and ideas leads to the relativizing of the role canon plays in biblical theology. For Barr, the events and concepts behind the text are truly where theology is to be found, so any text that gives record to these pretextual realities is fair game for doing biblical theology. Though the Apocrypha and the Dead Sea Scrolls provide historical and cultural detail that must be considered in any synthetic biblical theology, the fact that no modern community has defended the DSS as part of their canon must sound a cautionary note. There is historical as well as theological warrant for limiting biblical theology to the Christian canon, even if the parameters of such a canon are contested.

Finally, despite our appreciation for Barr's relative objectivity and willingness to reexamine theological convictions and assumptions in light of

---

34. Barr, *Concept*, 61.

historical and cultural research, he goes too far in sealing off what is a dialogical relationship between history and theology. Throughout his work Barr operates with a clear distinction between academic scholarship (ostensibly an intellectual activity) and religious devotion (an existential or liturgical activity). Barr would not allow for any devotional concerns to cloud his scholarly (and historical) approach to doing biblical theology. The high goal of scholarly objectivity and dispassionate historical discovery led Barr to bracket out his own personal faith and to insist that others do the same. Of course as faith commitments are moved or bracketed out, other commitments inevitably move in and take their place. To this end Barr's insistence on scholarly objectivity seems to have led to a methodological naturalism in his pursuit of the theology of the Bible.

Part 2

TYPE 2: BIBLICAL THEOLOGY AS HISTORY OF REDEMPTION

Chapter 3

BIBLICAL THEOLOGY AS HISTORY OF REDEMPTION: DEFINITION

The second type of biblical theology (BT2) relies on history to discern the normative purposes of God as unfolding through the Scriptures. Upon the continuum between history and theology, Biblical Theology as History of Redemption views God's revelation as a fundamentally progressive disclosure deployed along a sequential and historical timeline. D. A. Carson describes this type of biblical theology as "a discipline necessarily dependent on reading the Bible as an historically developing collection of documents."[1] While insisting on a "whole-Bible biblical theology," the way to discern this development is through tracing the major themes and overarching structural ideas through the whole of Scripture. Crucially, however, these themes and structural ideas are only discernable as they develop chronologically. The redeeming purposes of God, then, are viewed through the lens of God's *historically* progressing revelation; thus, BT2 is the History of Redemption. Brian Rosner argues:

> Biblical theology is principally concerned with the overall theological message of the whole Bible. It seeks to understand the parts in relation to the whole and, to achieve this, it must work with the mutual interaction of the literary, historical, and theological dimensions of the various corpora, and with the inter-relationships of these within the whole canon of Scripture.

---

1. D. A. Carson, "Current Issues in Biblical Theology: A New Testament Perspective," *BBR* 5 (1995): 27.

Biblical theology may be defined as theological interpretation of Scripture in and for the church. It proceeds with historical and literary sensitivity and seeks to analyse and synthesize the Bible's teaching about God and his relations to the world on its own terms, maintaining sight of the Bible's overarching narrative and Christocentric focus.[2]

As "interpretation of Scripture in and for the church," BT2 focuses on the meaning of the "parts" in relation to the "whole." Like BT3, which we will discuss in detail in chapter 5, there is a concern to balance history and theology, but whereas BT3 strikes the balance with the category of narrative, BT2 is more influenced by the concern to discover unity by the category of progressive history. Furthermore, it is telling that Rosner views biblical theology as balancing history, literature, and theology within "the various corpora" and "the whole canon" of Scripture.

As we will explore in more detail, concern for unity within discrete "corpora" as well as within the whole canon indicates various ways BT2 may be pursued. For some in BT2 (Roy Zuck and any number of OT or NT theologies), biblical theology is restricted by the historical context and literary unity of discrete sections of Scripture with any broader connections coming at the level of systematic theology (by contrast, BT1 would view systematic theology as a distinct and optional secondary task). Others within BT2 (e.g., Scott Hafemann and Elmer Martens) are happy to view the secondary move of relating the discrete corpora within Scripture as a whole to be *the* proper task of biblical theology.

THE TASK OF BIBLICAL THEOLOGY

The overall task of BT2 is to discern the coherence of the whole Bible as it unfolds over time. Like BT3, the key component of this task is the conviction that the Bible constitutes a single unified narrative; yet, distinct from BT3, this narrative develops historically via the sequence of God's redemptive purposes. Carson attempts his own definition of biblical theology:

Biblical theology, as its name implies, even as it works inductively from the diverse texts of the Bible, seeks to uncover and articulate the unity of all the biblical texts taken together, resorting primarily to the categories of those texts themselves. In this sense it is canonical biblical theology, "whole-Bible" biblical theology; i.e., its content is a theology of the whole Bible, not a theology that merely has roots in the Bible, or merely takes the Bible as the place to begin.[3]

---

2. Brian S. Rosner, "Biblical Theology," in *NDBT*, 3.
3. D. A. Carson, "Systematic and Biblical Theology," in *NDBT*, 94.

Carson stresses the unity of Scripture, highlighting biblical theology as "canonical biblical theology." But unlike BT4, Carson's use of "canonical" simply means a theology of the entire Bible, "'whole-Bible' biblical theology"; he is not referring to any complex notion of the formation of canon as we will consider for BT4. Furthermore, the unity of Scripture must surface through inductive study, using the categories of the texts themselves. Here biblical theology is dependent on exegetical analysis, which in turn is used to build toward greater and greater synthesis, ending ultimately in systematic theology. Stated succinctly, *the task of BT2 is to discern the historical progression of God's work of redemption through an inductive analysis of key themes developing through both discrete corpora and the whole of Scripture. Major themes such as covenant or kingdom constitute the theological connecting fibers between the Old and New Testaments, and these themes necessarily run along a historical trajectory, giving fundamental structure to the theology of the Bible.* This can be supported by several necessary explanations.

First, biblical theology consists of God's revelation of himself, his own self-disclosure. Biblical theology for both Carson and Rosner bears a family resemblance to the biblical theology of Geerhardus Vos. Vos occupied the newly created Chair of Biblical Theology at Princeton Seminary in 1892 and has exerted an enduring influence on the notion of biblical theology. He understood biblical theology as "that branch of Exegetical Theology which deals with the process of the self-revelation of God deposited in the Bible.... Biblical Theology deals with revelation as a divine activity, not as the finished product of that activity."[4] Thus, guided by this theological conviction, biblical theology is God's own self-disclosure.

Second, God's self-revelation is necessarily progressive. Reflecting on Vos's notion of biblical theology, Graeme Goldsworthy argues:

> God's revelation is embedded in history and involves a historic progressiveness ... biblical theology involves the quest for the big picture, or the overview, of biblical revelation. It is of the nature of biblical revelation that it tells a story rather than sets out timeless principles in abstract. They are given in an historical context of progressive revelation.[5]

As God's revelation progresses through the text of Scripture the "progressive" part of the revelation for BT2 is clearly historical progression. "God's revelation," Goldsworthy notes, is "embedded in history," which "involves a

---

4. Geerhardus Vos, *Biblical Theology* (Carlisle, PA: Banner of Truth Trust, 1975), 13.
5. Graeme Goldsworthy, *Preaching the Whole Bible as Christian Scripture* (Grand Rapids: Eerdmans, 2001), 22.

historic progressiveness."[6] Thus biblical theology's claim that God's revelation is progressive assumes *historical* progression.

This surfaces clearly as Goldsworthy contrasts biblical theology with systematic theology: "While systematic theology . . . is concerned with establishing the Christian doctrine of any given topic of the Bible, biblical theology is concerned with how the revelation of God was understood in its time, and what the total picture is that was built up over the whole historical process."[7] It is worth noting that like BT1, BT2 is concerned to understand God's revelation "in its time" and to maintain some distinction between biblical theology and systematic theology; yet unlike BT1, Goldsworthy would argue that God's progressive revelation is of direct (prescriptive) relevance to contemporary readers.

Finally, because biblical theology is the progressive (historical) self-disclosure of God himself, this revelation constitutes a unified message. Above all, Goldsworthy stresses that as progressive revelation Scripture is a coherent story—a "whole-Bible" biblical theology.

THE USE OF BIBLICAL THEOLOGY

For both BT1 and BT2, biblical theology is foundational for theology, but whereas theology is merely a further option for the pastor or theologian in BT1, BT2 senses a greater demand for biblical theology to be translated into theology for the church. As we saw above in Rosner's definition, BT2 is "in and for the church." Along with Rosner and Goldsworthy, D. A. Carson, Sidney Greidanus, and Edmund Clowney have all stressed the importance of biblical theology for the task of preaching the gospel.[8] So important is BT2 for the task of preaching that the significance of Jesus' redemption shrinks if it is dislocated from the overarching sweep of God's redemptive purposes viewed throughout the whole of Scripture. Goldsworthy notes:

---

6. Ibid., 22.
7. Ibid., 26. Goldsworthy notes the centrality of history for biblical theology elsewhere: "The essence of salvation-history is the recognition that the books of the Bible, while not being uniformly historical in form, all relate to an overarching history in which God acts to bring salvation to his people. Beginning at the creation event the story line moves through the entry of sin to the history of Israel as the chosen people. This history eventually leads to Jesus Christ and finally to the consummation and the new creation. The OT, then, is the first part of this story" (Graeme Goldsworthy, "Relationship of Old Testament and New Testament," in *NDBT*, 87).
8. For Carson's view of biblical theology and preaching, see the next chapter; see Sidney Greidanus, *The Modern Preacher and the Ancient Text: Interpreting and Preaching Biblical Literature* (Grand Rapids: Eerdmans, 1989); Edmund Clowney, *The Unfolding Mystery: Discovering Christ in the Old Testament* (Phillipsburg, NJ: Presbyterian & Reformed, 1991).

... biblical theology involves the quest for the big picture, or the overview of biblical revelation.... If we allow the Bible to tell its own story, we find a coherent and meaningful whole.... If God has given us a single picture of reality, albeit full of texture and variety, a picture spanning the ages, then our preaching must reflect the reality that is thus presented.[9]

Understanding one's current situation in the context of God's overarching redemptive purposes has long been an important part of Christian preaching. Therefore BT2, seen as reading Scripture with an eye to God's unfolding purposes throughout the ages, is primary to the direction and education of the church.

The importance of BT2 for preaching comes into sharpest focus as BT2 helps readers understand the Scriptures as God's message that shapes the reality of its readers. As a unified account of reality, the biblical story stands over against other versions of reality and thus serves as a clear warning against living out the values and goals of the surrounding culture. For Lesslie Newbigin, preaching announces God's reality and calls Christians to inhabit his story. "Preaching is the announcing of news," he argues; it is "the telling of a narrative. In a society that has a different story to tell about itself, preaching has to be firmly and unapologetically rooted in the real story."[10] Whereas BT3 would be in full agreement with Newbigin's assessment here, BT2 is distinct by limiting its investigation to the inductive movement and thematic development within the texts themselves. Furthermore, beyond the narrative concerns of BT3, BT2 views God's progressive revelation as the "real story" — that is, both rendering reality for readers and describing how the events actually played out in history.

Greidanus articulates the need to interpret any particular passage "in its broadest possible context, that is, Scripture's teaching regarding history as a whole." That is because,

Scripture teaches one universal kingdom history that encompasses all of created reality: past, present, and future ... its vision of history extends backward all the way to the beginning of time and forward all the way to the last day ... the biblical vision of history spans time from the first creation to the new creation, encompassing all of created reality.[11]

As the church announces the unified narrative of Scripture, it testifies to this reality. With regard to such preaching, Edmund Clowney notes:

---

9. Goldsworthy, *Preaching*, 22.
10. Lesslie Newbigin, "Missions," in *Concise Encyclopedia of Preaching* (ed. W. H. Willimon and R. Lischer; Louisville: Westminster John Knox, 1999), 336.
11. Greidanus, *The Modern Preacher*, 95.

> There are great stories in the Bible ... but it is possible to know Bible stories, yet miss *the* Bible story.... The Bible has a story line. It traces an unfolding drama. The story follows the history of Israel, but it does not begin there, nor does it contain what you would expect in a national history.... If we forget the story line ... we cut the heart out of the Bible.[12]

Thus theological education in the church embodied in the task of preaching is a central concern for BT2. BT2 is not only the task of the scholar, but also must be done by the pastor within the context of the church—specifically in the task of preaching.

THE SCOPE AND SOURCES OF BIBLICAL THEOLOGY

With respect to the sources for biblical theology, the sources for BT2 are *primarily* the texts of the Christian canon. Because BT2 is concerned with the progressive historical disclosure of God's purposes, this "special" or redemptive history is concerned with the actual historical events of the past. Therefore, whereas only the texts of the Christian canon are finally authoritative, extracanonical sources can be used to discern the historical contexts of the biblical texts. This historical research in turn situates the biblical texts within the redemptive historical trajectory so central to BT2.

Distinct from BT1, which is primarily concerned with descriptively tracing the sociological and religious development of Judaism and Christianity, BT2 seeks to discern the historical *and theological* revelation of God through a specific set of authoritative texts. Yet, even these texts must be understood by means of historical-grammatical analysis that will rely on extracanonical sources for such historical context. Whereas construction of BT2 is necessary for the Christian pastor to articulate the gospel fully, as demonstrated above, such a biblical theology is largely dependent on the task of scholarly research.

Not only should BT2 be founded on the books of the Christian canon; it must also be founded on *all* the books in the canon. This is, of course, to resist a canon within a canon. Karl Möller, commenting on Charles Scobie's biblical theology *Ways of our God*, notes this concern. Against what Scobie "regards as a strain of 'neo-Marcionism' in the work of scholars like Schleiermacher, von Harnack and Bultmann, Scobie stresses that biblical theology must attempt to do full justice to the Old Testament." Rather than limiting the "Old Testament to *Vetus Testamentum in novo receptum*, he contends that

---

12. Clowney, *The Unfolding Mystery*, 11 (emphasis original).

biblical theology must deal with *Vetus Testamentum per se*."[13] Otherwise said, a proper biblical theology ought not limit itself to hearing the "Old Testament as received in the new" but as the "Old Testament in itself." Biblical theology, then, must be more than just the sum of OT and NT theologies. Rather, it must be concerned with the entire canon, and always be awake to the danger of both a canon within the canon and the tendency to shrink the OT merely to its reception in the NT.

For Goldsworthy the unity of the Old and New Testaments fundamentally rests on theological conviction:

> The unity of the Bible is [a] matter of revelation, not of empirical investigation.... The unity of the Bible is an article of faith before ever it is arrived at empirically. The empirical discovery of the unity is governed by the presupposition of divine revelation.[14]

Though he stresses the theological priority of biblical unity, Goldsworthy proceeds to offer historical-grammatical evidence for the unifying theme of kingdom stretching through the entire canon.[15] This illustrates BT2's commitment to Scripture alone while still using extracanonical sources to establish the historical context of those inspired texts.

THE HERMENEUTICAL APPROACH OF BIBLICAL THEOLOGY

Biblical theology as the history of redemption implies a set of hermeneutical commitments. Goldsworthy notes: "An evangelical biblical theology

---

13. Karl Möller, "The Nature and Genre of Biblical Theology: Some Reflections in the Light of Charles H. H. Scobie's 'Prolegomena to Biblical Theology,'" in *Out of Egypt: Biblical Theology and Biblical Interpretation* (ed. Craig Bartholomew et al.; SHS 5; Grand Rapids: Zondervan, 2004), 148–50.

14. Goldsworthy, *Preaching*, 22–23. Compare this with Bauckham's argument for an internal empirical unity to Scripture: "For warrant to do this [to read Scripture as a unitary story], we do not need to rely solely on the mere existence of the canon or the church's tradition of reading it, nor need we make a simple arbitrary decision to read Scripture in this way, but we can appeal to significant features of the texts themselves" ("Reading Scripture as a Coherent Story," in *The Art of Reading Scripture* [ed. Ellen F. Davis and Richard B. Hays; Grand Rapids: Eerdmans, 2003], 42). Bauckham offers compelling textual evidence that Scripture may be read as a coherent narrative. Though Bauckham does not address Goldsworthy directly, he continues in a note: "I am less happy than Loughlin to rely on the church's 'traditional reading rules' (doctrines) for reading Scripture as a unity without also seeking what there is about Scripture that makes such rules appropriate" (ibid, 42 n.6).

15. Goldsworthy offers a comprehensive and exegetically astute account of how the gospel is the overarching subject matter of Scripture—providing an explicitly empirical account of the Bible's unity—in *The Goldsworthy Trilogy: Gospel and Kingdom; Gospel in Wisdom; The Gospel in Revelation* (Milton Keys, UK: Paternoster, 2000).

expresses confidence in the integrity of the biblical text and its historical perspective."[16] God's revelation points readers to the real events of history, but a history that is invested with meaning. Rather than a string of unrelated events, redemptive history is the unified and progressive (historical) account of God's saving purposes in and for the world. The hermeneutical convictions of BT2 come to the surface in the following key characteristics.

First, because of the dependence on historical development, the Bible must be read as *progressive* revelation. That is, any one passage must be read not only in its specific context, but also as the next step in God's story of redemption. Craig Bartholomew and Michael Goheen describe the progressive nature of revelation as "an epochal structure" of Christian Scripture.[17] Whether from covenant to covenant or dispensation to dispensation, the conviction is that God has progressively revealed his purposes through the events of history. Each movement in the progressive unfolding of God's work in redemption reveals true aspects of God's character and the fallen condition of humanity. This is to insist that every stage in revelation is a discrete moment in the redemption story that is both irreducible and necessary within the movement of God's progressive communication.

As a hermeneutical principle this requires that each passage of Scripture be understood in its micro (or immediate) context. Because each progressive moment is indeed God's revelation, each passage must be understood within its historical, literary, and cultural context. Discerning what the author meant to communicate to the original audience aids the modern reader in hearing God's progressive revelation in a particular moment in redemptive history. For all forms of BT2, this constitutes a primary starting point.

A second hermeneutical guide is that the Bible is a *progressive unity*. Though made up of historically and culturally discrete texts, the entire canon constitutes a single, coherent narrative so that the Bible must be interpreted in light of the overarching biblical story.[18] Thus any individual text cannot exist as a free-floating moral story or theological principle, but must be interpreted as a discernable segment of a forward-moving narrative whole. BT2 insists that a reader place each text not only into its historical-cultural context but also in the overarching context of God's story of redemption. That is, each text must be read in light of its macro-context. Each passage fits within the

---

16. Goldsworthy, *Preaching*, 27. He continues: "'Salvation history' is a term that has come to be used in relation to a certain perspective in doing biblical theology, one that recognizes a specific history as the framework within which God has worked, is now working, and will work in the future."

17. Craig Bartholomew and Michael Goheen, "Story and Biblical Theology," in *Out of Egypt*, 148–50.

18. Goldsworthy, *Preaching*, 98.

Bible's overarching story that has as its purpose the revelation of Christ as the climax of all God's redeeming activity in history.

Yet among proponents of BT2 there is not complete agreement as to whether this second step is just that, a step or a leap. Does this second step mean that a passage from Romans must be placed within the larger corpus of Paul's writings? Or does it require understanding the same passage from Romans in light of Isaiah, or the entire Genesis-to-Revelation story of Scripture? While noting the hermeneutical importance of progression and unity (or micro- and macro-context), there is a variety of ways proponents of BT2 understand how these work in forming biblical theology. The key issue is the degree of synthesis in placing the passage in its macro-context. For some within BT2 the macro-context simply requires setting a passage within its larger corpus (the Gospels, Paul's letters, etc.). For others the macro-context remains incomplete until the passage is set within its overarching canonical context.

In an attempt to account for some of this variety within BT2, we discern three identifiable schools of thought, which we will call the "Dallas school," the "Chicago school," and the "Philadelphia school."[19] These "schools" represent slightly different methodologies within BT2 and run along a rough spectrum. Though clearly distinguished here, these "schools" in fact share much in common. Below we have clearly distinguished them one from another for the purpose of foregrounding the variations within BT2.

Dallas School

Starting at one end of the spectrum, the "Dallas school" of biblical theology is most concerned to articulate the theology running through an individual book or collections of books within the canon. Working inductively from the text, proponents of this approach move from the micro-context of each passage to produce an account of the theological content of each book, ultimately building toward a theology of the Gospels or a theology of Paul.[20] The emphasis (and strength) of this view centers on exegetical analysis.

The reason this variation of BT2 is labeled the "Dallas school" is because a group of scholars from Dallas Theological Seminary have published and propagated a methodology that aims at inductively surfacing theological

---

19. Thanks are due to Ken Way who in conversation sparked the initial idea of categorizing various groups within BT2 this way.

20. Goldsworthy notes: "One approach to biblical theology concentrates on the theological content of each of the biblical books or, perhaps, corpora. Thus we arrive at the theology of the Pentateuch, the Former Prophets, the different prophetic books, and so on.... Such an analytical approach is valid and necessary, but it needs to be linked with a synthetic perspective that relates each individual part to the whole" (*Preaching*, 26).

themes at a book and corpus level. In two volumes entitled *A Biblical Theology of the Old Testament* and *A Biblical Theology of the New Testament*, the same group of scholars from DTS attempts to "survey the Bible as a whole from an analytical and inductive stance and to extract from it those themes and emphases that are inherent to it and that recur with such regularity and in such evident patterns as to generate their own theological rubrics."[21]

The Dallas school focuses on the integrity of any particular passage in its immediate historical context. The constraining concerns of the historical author and audience focus the kind of theological themes found within the text. Only when these historically discrete "theologies" are set end-to-end does a truly "whole-Bible biblical theology" come into focus. In other words, this approach implicitly treats biblical theology as a clearly distinguishable step between grammatical-historical exegesis and systematic theology. Biblical theology ends up as a bridge linking lexical-historical analysis to systematic theology's more synthetic task.

This approach finds strength in its inductive work from the text; it pays close and careful attention to and does justice to micro-context. Like BT1, the Dallas school focuses on clear description while at the same time resisting the tendency in BT1 to reduce the text merely to its historical background. Finally, rather than establishing connections between texts by subjective connections arising from a premature use of theology, the inductive foundation to biblical theology is supported by clearly demonstrated themes and repeated terms found within the texts.

Chicago School

The second school within BT2 is the "Chicago school." This school of biblical theology enjoys a host of advocates. First, it finds representation above in Carson's definition of biblical theology and in a monograph series for which Carson is series editor: New Studies in Biblical Theology. Because Carson is such a prolific author and has for so long been Professor of New Testament at Trinity Evangelical Divinity School in Chicago, we have labeled this the "Chicago school." In the preface to the New Studies in Biblical Theology series Carson notes:

> Contributions to the series focus on one or more of three areas: 1. The nature and status of biblical theology ...; 2. The articulation and exposition of the structure of thought of a particular biblical writer or corpus [the Dallas school, above]; and 3. The delineation of a biblical theme across all or part of the biblical corpora.

---

21. Eugene H. Merrill, "Introduction," in *A Biblical Theology of the Old Testament* (ed. Roy B. Zuck; Chicago: Moody Press, 1991), 3. The other volume, also edited by Roy B. Zuck, is *A Biblical Theology of the New Testament* (Chicago: Moody Press, 1994).

Clearly there are significant points of correspondence between Dallas and Chicago. The second area of investigation for NSBT rests firmly within the Dallas emphasis. Yet, with the third area the Chicago school merges away from Dallas to attempt a synthesis beyond the corpus-level to consider the entire Bible. Whereas Dallas is concerned for whole-Bible analysis and will produce thematic studies cutting across the entire canon, most in the Dallas school consider book or corpus-level analysis the task of biblical theology and would leave whole-Bible synthesis to systematic theology.[22] Though Dallas's position echoes that of BT1 in relegating canon-wide synthesis to systematic theology, such synthesis is needed not only to produce an accurate picture of what ancient peoples believed about God (BT1), but further is necessary for modern believers to synthesize and apply the prescriptive teaching of Scripture.

Another group working within the Chicago school, especially with the analysis of biblical themes, has provided several excellent examples of the Chicago approach in an edited volume called *Central Themes in Biblical Theology*. Editors Scott Hafemann and Paul House offer a collection exploring "whole-Bible" biblical theology.[23] Each of these studies takes as their starting point the classic definition of biblical theology offered by Elmer Martens: "Biblical theology investigates the themes presented in Scripture and defines their inter-relationships. Biblical theology is an attempt to get to the theological heart of the Bible."[24]

On the one hand, rather than working from a theology of Isaiah or Matthew and then building up to a larger theology of the entire Bible, the Chicago school understands biblical theology as identifying the key themes that come directly from the text and connect the diverse texts of the Bible. Here the

---

22. Even where Dallas moves on to systematic theology proper and offers a whole-Bible synthesis, a degree of discontinuity remains that is not characteristic of the Chicago school. As a generalization, the Dallas type of whole-Bible synthesis is informed by a dispensational hermeneutic (whether classic or progressive), which is much more attuned to the discontinuities between biblical corpora and Testaments, whereas the Chicago school views whole-Bible synthesis as properly a task of biblical theology and generates a type of synthesis that generally stresses greater continuities between corpora and the Testaments.

23. Scott J. Hafemann and Paul R. House, eds., *Central Themes in Biblical Theology: Mapping Unity in Diversity* (Grand Rapids: Baker, 2007). Scobie defines this as the "thematic approach" to biblical theology: "A thematic approach to Biblical Theology seeks to structure its treatment around themes or topics which arise from the biblical material itself rather than being imposed upon it on the basis of a predetermined dogmatic system" ("The Structure of Biblical Theology," *TynBul* 42 [1991]: 173). See also Charles H. H. Scobie, *The Ways of Our God: An Approach to Biblical Theology* (Grand Rapids: Eerdmans, 2003), 46–48, 85–87. See also the work of Thielman, Marshall, and Köstenberger.

24. Elmer A. Martens, "Tackling Old Testament Theology," *JETS* 20 (1977): 123; quoted in Hafemann and House, *Central Themes in Biblical Theology*, 16.

Chicago school moves beyond Dallas in that for Carson biblical theology "is canonical biblical theology, 'whole-Bible' biblical theology; i.e. its content is a theology of the whole Bible."[25] Rosner argues that biblical theology "seeks to understand the parts in relation to the whole." Though using historical and literary tools, it "seeks to analyse and synthesize the Bible's teaching about God and his relations to the world on its own terms, maintaining sight of the Bible's overarching narrative and Christocentric focus."[26] As we will briefly consider in the following chapter, typology is a primary tool for the Chicago school in establishing connections across corpora and Testaments within Scripture. Thus the Chicago school moves beyond describing the theology of Isaiah or Matthew and attempts to articulate the thematic coherence of the Bible as a whole.

On the other hand, the Chicago school still views biblical theology as a "bridge discipline," sequentially linking exegesis to systematic theology. Carson argues that as a discipline, biblical theology "stands closer to the text than systematic theology, aims to achieve genuine sensitivity with respect to the distinctiveness of each corpus, and seeks to connect the diverse corpora using their own categories." And because biblical theology is situated in closer proximity to the text, he argues that "biblical theology stands as a kind of bridge discipline between responsible exegesis and responsible systematic theology."[27] Whereas for Dallas whole-Bible synthesis is necessary for correct understanding of Scripture, it is the task of systematic theology. In Dallas once a student asks, "What does the whole Bible say about 'x'?" they have moved from biblical theology to systematic theology proper. For Chicago, however, there is an interconnected progression from exegesis through biblical theology to systematic theology, where biblical theology serves as a "bridge" between the two.

Philadelphia School

Finally, the "Philadelphia school" of biblical theology moves more aggressively toward macro-context synthesis and maintains a more integrated relationship between biblical theology and systematic theology. Bartholomew and Goheen observe, "There is a 'redemptive-historical' school that developed in the Netherlands from the late nineteenth century and reached its zenith in the twentieth century between the world wars. This tradition is not broadly known but is rich in resources for biblical theology."[28] The name comes from

---

25. Carson, "Systematic and Biblical Theology," in *NDBT*, 94.
26. Rosner, "Biblical Theology," in *NDBT*, 3.
27. Carson, "Systematic and Biblical Theology," in *NDBT*, 94.
28. Bartholomew and Goheen, "Story and Biblical Theology," 153.

a discernable trajectory in interpretation connecting back to the Reformation (the federal/covenant theology of the seventeenth century)[29] through Dutch neo-Calvinism of the nineteenth century (Herman Bavink and Abraham Kuyper; and Herman Ridderbos[30] in the twentieth century) largely centered in the Theological University in Kampen.[31]

This tradition found particular articulation in the United States at Princeton (G. Vos) and finally in places like Westminster Theological Seminary in Philadelphia (John Murray and Richard Gaffin).[32] The Philadelphia school stands in the long tradition that understands Scripture as a unified, unfolding narrative about God's action in the world to bring about the redemption of all things. As early as Irenaeus, interpreters clearly understood the narrative whole or the "story" shape of Scripture. Augustine, Calvin, and Jonathan Edwards all wrote about the unified structure of the Scripture using some form of what might be described as biblical theology.[33] We will see that this tradition loosely connects to Narrative Biblical Theology (BT3), although it precedes the contemporary stress on literature and narrative theology.[34]

---

29. Scobie notes: "The thematic approach [our BT2] is in general a relatively modern one, though it should be noted that recognition of 'covenant' as a key theme of Biblical Theology has deep roots in Reformed theology especially in the thought of Johannes Cocceius (1603–1669) whose work laid the basis for the influential federal or covenant theology. Cocceius did not follow the standard outline of topics but organized his theological system around a theme derived directly from the Bible, that of the covenant. He distinguished the covenant of works *(foedus operum)* or covenant of nature *(foedus naturae)* in operation before the fall, the covenant of grace *(foedus gratiae)* operative thereafter. Within the latter, two (or in some forms of federal theology, three) economies or dispensations were distinguished, so that thereby elements of a historical scheme were also included" ("The Structure of Biblical Theology," *TynBul* 42 [1991], 174).

30. See books by H. Ridderbos, *When the Time Had Fully Come: Studies in New Testament Biblical Theology* (Grand Rapids: Eerdmans, 1957); *Redemptive History and the New Testament Scriptures* (trans. H. de Jongste; Phillipsburg, NJ: Presbyterian & Reformed, 1988); *The Coming of the Kingdom* (trans. H. de Jongste; Philadelphia: Presbyterian & Reformed, 1962); *Paul: An Outline of His Theology* (trans. John R. De Witt; Grand Rapids: Eerdmans, 1975).

31. Kampen is a city in Holland that is home to the Theological University known for a strict Dutch neo-Calvinism in the nineteenth century.

32. For the Vos–Murray trajectory, see Richard B. Gaffin Jr., "Systematic and Biblical Theology," *WTJ* 38 (1976): 281–99. There are other scholars and institutions that stand in this tradition to various degrees. For example, the extremely influential work of Oscar Cullman would generally register here along with institutions like Calvin College and Seminary (Grand Rapids, MI) and Western Theological Seminary (Holland, MI). Though Cullman merits extensive treatment on his own for purposes of clarity and simplicity, we have left discussion of his contribution for a different context. G. K. Beal has attempted to extend the tradition of Vos in his recent work, *A New Testament Biblical Theology: The Unfolding of the Old Testament in the New* (Grand Rapids: Baker, 2011).

33. See J. V. Fesko's argument that this version of biblical theology can be traced to the early church, "On the Antiquity of Biblical Theology," in *Resurrection & Eschatology: Theology in Service of the Church: Essays in Honor of Richard B. Gaffin Jr.* (ed. Lane G. Tipton and Jeffery C. Waddington; Phillipsburg, NJ: Presbyterian & Reformed, 2008), 443–77.

34. See Bartholomew and Goheen, "Story and Biblical Theology," 153.

What distinguishes the Philadelphia school from the Chicago school is that beyond discerning the themes that come from and in turn unite Scripture, the Philadelphia school understands the whole of biblical theology as greater than the sum of its parts. Not only does the Philadelphia school attempt to understand how the grand themes of Scripture unite across the canon, but it also attempts to discern how each of these themes comes to a single climax in Jesus Christ. Though the Chicago school discerns a christocentric focus in the grand sweep of biblical themes, the Philadelphia school is guided by christological concern from start to finish — it is both the starting confession and the final goal. More so than the others, the Philadelphia school views biblical theology as redemptive-historical at its heart.

Again, there is a degree of permeability between Chicago and Philadelphia on this point. For example, the Chicago school would also be self-aware of reading Scripture in a redemptive-historical way. Yet for the Philadelphia school, biblical theology is more than the sum of theological themes running through the text; it constitutes an overarching theological superstructure for the biblical story. Thus biblical theology is more than a "bridge." The center focus of this superstructure is Jesus himself. The Philadelphia school argues that this focus is *theologically* (i.e., hermeneutically) *required* because all Scripture is about Jesus (Luke 24:44 – 47). Another way of expressing this particularity of the Philadelphia school is to say that whereas for Dallas and Chicago biblical theology is regulated by the preliminary step of exegesis, for the Philadelphia school, biblical theology regulates the exegetical task itself.[35]

That all of Scripture is about Jesus is not only the empirical conclusion of tracing the Bible's thematic trajectories; it also serves as a hermeneutical lens for understanding the purpose and subject matter of the Bible itself. Vos, for example, understood the overarching subject matter of biblical theology as Christ himself:

> From the beginning all redeeming acts of God aim at the creation and introduction of this new organic principle, which is none other than Christ. All Old Testament redemption is but the saving activity of God working toward the realization of this goal, the great supernatural prelude to the Incarnation and the Atonement.[36]

---

35. On this point see especially Gaffin, "Systematic and Biblical Theology," 293. As we will see in the next chapter, Carson, as representing the Chicago school, acknowledges biblical theology or systematic theology's influence on exegesis; nevertheless, he concludes that exegesis is the necessary first step in interpretation and must be kept free from the controlling influence of systematic theology.
36. Geerhardus Vos, *The Idea of Biblical Theology as a Science and as a Theological Discipline* (New York: Anson D. F. Randolph, 1894), 12.

Goldsworthy also notes along these lines:

> The soundest methodological starting point is the gospel since the person of Jesus is proclaimed as the final and fullest expression of God's revelation of his kingdom. Jesus is the goal and fulfillment of the whole Old Testament and, as the embodiment of the truth of God, he is the interpretative key of the Bible.[37]

Though there are resonances here with BT5, Goldsworthy's hermeneutic with Jesus as the key is still mediated via the historical development of redemption history. In other words, though Jesus is the key, history remains the overarching structure.

Each of these schools has a particular view of the relationship between biblical theology and systematic theology. We have already seen in the introduction to this book how Vos insists, unlike Dallas or Chicago, that biblical theology and systematic theology are sibling disciplines. Vos elaborates on this insight by claiming that "Dogmatic Theology is, when rightly cultivated, as truly a Biblical and as truly an inductive science as its younger sister."[38] Vos continues:

> And the latter [biblical theology] needs a constructive principle for arranging her facts as well as the former. The only difference is, that in the one case this constructive principle is systematic and logical, whereas in the other case it is purely historical. In others words, Systematic Theology endeavors to construct a circle, Biblical Theology seeks to reproduce a line.[39]

Fesko notes the close connection between biblical theology and systematic theology as well: "Systematic and biblical theology are *synoptic*.... They are like stereo vision; apart from one another the Scriptures are two-dimensional, but together they appear three-dimensional." He concludes, "to borrow a famous illustration, while we may distinguish the rays of the sun from its heat, we cannot separate them. Likewise, we may distinguish biblical from systematic theology, but we must never separate them: the *ordo* and *historia salutis* are inseparably conjoined."[40]

---

37. Goldsworthy, *Preaching*, 25. See more Goldsworthy, *According to Plan: The Unfolding Revelation of God in the Bible* (Leicester, UK: Inter-Varsity Press, 1991).
38. It should be pointed out that both Dallas and Chicago would reserve the term "inductive" as a characteristic of biblical theology alone.
39. Geerhardus Vos, "The Idea of Biblical Theology as a Science and as a Theological Discipline," in *Redemptive History and Biblical Interpretation: The Shorter Writings of Geerhardus Vos* (Phillipsburg, NJ: Presbyterian and Reformed, 2001), 23.
40. Fesko, "On the Antiquity," 475–76. Fesko continues on the same page referring to J. Gresham Machen's convocation address at Westminster Theological Seminary in 1929: "It must not be thought that systematic theology is one whit less biblical than biblical theology is. But is differs from biblical theology in that, standing on the foundation of biblical theology, it seeks to set forth, no longer in the order of the time when it was revealed, but in order of logical relationships, the grand sum of what God has told us in his Word.... We believe for our part that God has spoken to us in his Word, and that he has given us not merely theology, but a system of theology, a great logically consistent body of truth."

THE SUBJECT MATTER OF
BIBLICAL THEOLOGY

Rather than historical description (BT1) or narrative coherence (BT3), the subject matter of BT2 is the progressive unity of God's redemptive acts as revealed in the Christian canon. Even among the various schools of BT2 noted above, they all hold that in word and event, the Old and New Testaments are the special revelation of God and that God's self-revelation is progressive through a "special" history and reaches its climax in Jesus Christ. Even though in the Philadelphia school we noted the centrality of Jesus in the interpretive process, this christological fabric is stretched out over the framework of progressive historical development. This is "special" history—that is, redemptive history. Richard Gaffin, standing within the Philadelphia school as we have defined it, notes:

> ... the proper focus of interpretation is the subject matter of the text, that is, the *history* with Christ at its center that *lies in back of the text*. With a view to its content, then, a primary and essential qualification of the unity of the Bible is that that unity is redemptive-historical. *The context that ultimately controls the understanding of a given text is* not a literary framework or pattern of relationships but *the historical structure of the revelation* process itself. In the final analysis the analogy of Scripture is the analogy of parts in an historically unfolding and differentiating organism.[41]

Whether seen from Dallas, Chicago, or Philadelphia, the subject matter of BT2 is the progressive history of God's actions across both Old and New Testaments. This progressive history reaches its climax in the revelation of Jesus Christ and is most clearly discerned via the unfolding historical development of God's story of redemption. Therefore, the progressive unity of God's redemptive acts coming to a climax in Jesus Christ is the subject matter of BT2.

CONCLUSION

The clear strength of BT2 is its exegetically driven and historically sensitive reading of Scripture. Upon the continuum between history and theology, BT2 relies on redemptive history to discern the normative purposes of God as they unfold through the Scriptures (theology). Though there are at least three different "schools" within this one type of biblical theology, BT2 in general

---

41. Gaffin, "Systematic and Biblical Theology," 293–94 (emphasis added).

views God's revelation as a fundamentally progressive disclosure deployed along a sequential and historical timeline. The central means to discern this redemptive history is through inductive analysis of key themes that develop through both discrete corpora and the whole of Scripture.

Chapter 4

BIBLICAL THEOLOGY AS HISTORY OF REDEMPTION: D. A. CARSON

D. A. Carson serves as an apt example of doing Biblical Theology as the History of Redemption. In a recent article, Andrew Naselli observes that "though Carson has written an unusual number of works that are directly or indirectly related to theological method, he has not yet written one that systematically presents his theological method as a package."[1] Naselli goes on to offer a helpful overview of Carson's interpretive process. Here we are most particularly concerned with how Carson's methodology highlights Biblical Theology as History of Redemption (BT2).

Donald Arthur (D. A.) Carson (b. 1946) was raised in Drummondville, Quebec, to parents of Irish descent (his father was born near Belfast). He attended McGill University in Montreal from 1963 to 1967, graduating with a bachelor's degree in chemistry and mathematics. He then earned a master's in divinity from Central Baptist Seminary in Toronto. After serving as pastor of Richmond Baptist Church in Richmond, British Columbia, he enrolled at Emmanuel College, Cambridge, where he wrote his Ph.D. in New Testament under the direction of Barnabas Lindars. In 1977 Carson joined the faculty of Trinity Evangelical Divinity School in Chicago, where he continues to serve as Research Professor of New Testament.

---

1. Andrew Naselli, "D. A. Carson's Theological Method," *SBET* 29/2 (2011): 245–74, 245. We are very grateful to Andy for sharing with us an early version of his article.

Carson is a particularly apt figure to consider here because of his broad influence within evangelicalism. Almost everyone in the evangelical world is aware of his influence not only in NT studies, but also in hermeneutics, linguistics, systematic theology, and pastoral theology. He has served on the faculty at a major evangelical seminary for over thirty years; he has been book review editor for the *Journal of Evangelical Theological Society*; he has served as the editor of the *Trinity Journal*; and, in addition to authoring or editing over sixty books himself, he is the series editor for three major projects: the Pillar Commentary on the New Testament, New Studies in Biblical Theology, and Studies in the Biblical Greek. In addition to shaping evangelical academics, Carson's influence is palpably felt in the church. A tireless conference speaker for churches and campus ministries, Carson regularly teaches and preaches around the world. And more recently he has encouraged cooperation among gospel-centered ministries by serving as president and cofounder of The Gospel Coalition. Andreas Köstenberger notes:

> D. A. Carson may one day be remembered as one of the last great Renaissance men in evangelical biblical scholarship. In an age of increasing specialization and fragmentation, Carson, to the admiring disbelief of many of his colleagues, persistently refuses to limit his interests. His publications cover a vast range of subjects: New Testament Greek, Bible translation, hermeneutics, contextualization, the use of the Old Testament in the New, preaching, various aspects of New Testament and biblical theology, major commentaries on Matthew and John, and even poetry.[2]

It is especially this interdisciplinary commitment that has equipped Carson for his many forays into biblical theology.

BIBLICAL THEOLOGY: A "BRIDGE" DISCIPLINE

Acknowledging that biblical theology is notoriously difficult to define as an academic discipline, Carson observes that at "one level, there cannot be a 'right' or 'wrong' definition of biblical theology." Further he notes: "the history of 'biblical theology' is extraordinarily diverse. Everyone does that which is right in his or her own eyes, and calls it biblical theology."[3] Granting this degree of plasticity to biblical theology, he enumerates several key

---

2. Andreas Köstenberger, "D. A. Carson: His Life and Work to Date," in *Understanding the Times: New Testament Studies in the 21ˢᵗ Century: Essays in Honor of D. A. Carson on the Occasion of this 65ᵗʰ Birthday* (Wheaton, IL: Crossway, 2011), 357.
3. Carson, "Systematic and Biblical Theology," 91.

characteristics that give greater "clarity of thought" to biblical theology as a discrete discipline.[4]

We will consider these key characteristics of biblical theology below, but first we will offer an overview of Carson's notion of biblical theology especially with regard to how it relates as part of a larger complex of exegetical and theological disciplines. As we have already discovered, Carson understands biblical theology as a "bridge discipline between responsible exegesis and responsible systematic theology (even though each of these inevitably influences the other two)."[5] Thus biblical theology finds its definition via its relationship with other discrete disciplines in the interpretive process.

Conceding that modern academic overspecialization drives the following elements apart, Carson argues that exegesis, biblical theology, historical theology, and systematic theology should remain meaningfully connected — discrete steps in an integrated process of biblical interpretation. While interrelated and integrated, the logical progression of these disciplines, for Carson, consistently moves in one particular direction. This progression begins with exegesis; then, developing along the historical progression of God's revelation, exegesis gives way to biblical theology. The historically developing structure of biblical theology then builds the foundation for historical and finally systematic theology. The following diagram summarizes Carson's understanding of the progression of these discrete steps:

Exegesis → Biblical Theology → [Historical Theology] → Systematic Theology[6]

Carson is careful to nuance this string of relationships away from an overly simplistic linear progression. "In fact," he notes, "this paradigm, though neat, is naïve. No exegesis is ever done in a vacuum. If every theist is in some sense a systematician, then he is a systematician *before* he begins his exegesis."[7] Here Carson wisely points out the interpreter's presuppositions, including theological presuppositions, which influence one's search for meaning even prior to exegetical analysis. While moving forward developmentally from exegesis to systematic theology, Carson notes that each step of the progression "feeds back," as it were, on the previous steps. Thus one's findings in biblical

---

4. Carson, "Current Issues," 27.
5. Carson, "Systematic and Biblical Theology," 94.
6. D. A. Carson, "Unity and Diversity in the New Testament," in D. A. Carson and John D. Woodbridge, *Scripture and Truth* (Grand Rapids: Baker, 1992), 91. Carson explains that "the brackets around the third element are meant to suggest that in this paradigm historical theology makes a direct contribution to the development from biblical theology to systematic theology but is not itself a part of that line" (91).
7. Ibid., 91–92 (emphasis original).

theology will feed back on and influence exegesis; one's systematic formulations will feed back on biblical theology, and so forth.

Yet, after offering this careful nuance, in the end Carson concludes:

> Nevertheless the line of final control is the straight one from exegesis right through biblical and historical theology to systematic theology. The final authority is the Scriptures, and the Scriptures alone. For this reason exegesis, though affected by systematic theology, is not to be shackled by it.[8]

That is, because the Christian Scriptures alone are authoritative, exegesis of Scripture is necessarily the first step in accurate interpretation. Therefore, exegesis, though influenced by theology, is not in the end "to be shackled" by systematic theology. While offering a helpful emphasis on the text of Scripture bearing final authority, Carson seems to flatten his carefully nuanced position above.

Here especially one can detect the way in which Carson understands biblical theology as a bridge discipline from exegesis to systematic theology. It necessarily stands in the interval between exegesis of the text and the systematic formulation of doctrine. Though "affected by systematic theology," the subject matter of exegesis is the text itself; thus exegesis holds a primacy over the sequence of other tasks. For Carson, biblical theology

> mediates the influence of biblical exegesis on systematic theology. Within the limits already set forth, just as systematic theology partially constrains and ideally enriches exegesis, so also does it serve biblical theology. More importantly, biblical theology more immediately constrains and enriches exegesis than systematic theology can do.[9]

Here Carson understands that biblical theology is impossible without exegesis as its antecedent analytical foundation. For Carson, "exegesis tends to focus on analysis" and biblical theology "tends towards synthesis."[10] Naselli articulates Carson's notion well: "Exegesis controls biblical theology, and biblical theology influences exegesis."[11] The relationship between exegesis and biblical theology is rather clear: exegesis, in the end, exerts a controlling influence on the formation of biblical theology that biblical theology cannot fully reciprocate.

---

8. Ibid.
9. D. A. Carson, "The Role of Exegesis in Systematic Theology," in *Doing Theology in Today's World: Essays in Honor of Kenneth S. Kantzer* (ed. John D. Woodbridge and Thomas E. McComisky; Grand Rapids: Zondervan, 1994), 39–76 (66).
10. D. A. Carson "Systematic Theology and Biblical Theology," in *NDBT*, 89–100 (91).
11. Naselli, "Carson's Theological Method," 264.

A biblical theology fully founded on the prior activity of exegesis in turn informs systematic formulation of Scripture's content. Carson understands that systematic theology "will inevitably be logical, primarily atemporal, and with appropriate reflection as to what it means for us today." By contrast, biblical theology is characterized by historical development as an "organic growth."[12] Systematic theology "answers primarily atemporal questions," addressing "the contemporary age at the most crucial junctures"; biblical theology "works inductively from the biblical text; the text itself sets the agenda." Further, biblical theology seeks "to deploy categories and pursue an agenda set by the text itself."[13] What is apparent from this contrast between biblical theology and systematic theology is that, for Carson, biblical theology is clearly nestled closer to the text of Scripture.

In other words, systematic theology tends to be a little further removed from the biblical text than does biblical theology, but it is a little closer to cultural engagement. Biblical theology tends to seek out the rationality and communicative genius of each literary genre; systematic theology tends to integrate the diverse rationalities in its pursuit of large-scale, worldview-forming synthesis. In this sense, systematic theology tends to be a culminating discipline; biblical theology, though it is a worthy end in itself, tends to be a bridge discipline.[14]

Though Carson acknowledges that systematic theology regularly feeds back on exegesis and biblical theology, in the end, systematic theology depends on the structuring insights of biblical theology as biblical theology progresses "inductively from the biblical text." Carson understands that "the text itself sets the agenda" for the task of biblical theology, where the actual subject matter of systematic theology is "at a second or third or fourth order of remove from Scripture, as it engages, say, philosophical and scientific questions not directly raised by the biblical texts themselves."[15]

Rather than a "bridge to nowhere," Carson understands biblical theology as *the only* bridge spanning the exegesis–systematic theology gap. Naselli summarizes this point using Carson's own vocabulary: "Systematic theology must build on biblical theology's 'syntheses of biblical corpora' and 'tracing of the Bible's story-line' with the result that 'each major strand' of systematic theology will 'be woven into the fabric that finds its climax and ultimate significance in the person and work of Jesus Christ.'"[16]

---

12. Carson, "Exegesis in Systematic Theology," 65, 64.
13. Carson, "Current Issues," 29.
14. Carson, "Systematic Theology and Biblical Theology," 103.
15. Carson, "Current Issues," 29.
16. Naselli, "Carson's Theological Method," 267.

CARSON'S "KEYS" TO USEFUL
BIBLICAL THEOLOGY

Having considered Carson's overarching placement of biblical theology, we turn now to consider the key characteristics that clarify biblical theology such that it might be a useful tool in interpretation. First, because biblical theology must not be identified or confused with systematic theology, *"biblical theology is a discipline necessarily dependent on reading the Bible as an historically developing collection of documents."*[17] Following Ladd,[18] Carson insists that chronological development is necessary for biblical theology as "holy history" (*Heilsgeschichte*). As we saw in the previous chapter, BT2 characteristically holds that historical progression of God's self-revelation constitutes biblical theology. Specifically, a biblical-theological investigation is constituted by "salvation-historical study of the biblical texts (i.e., the understanding and exposition of the texts along their chronological line of development)."[19] This is characteristic of BT2 as a whole.

Second, for Carson, biblical theology must be founded on a *"coherent and agreed canon."*[20] This is another characteristic of BT2 noted in the previous chapter. Here biblical theology not only limits its theological reflection and formulation to the Christian canon, but also ensures that all the texts of that canon are equally used in a coherent fashion for theological reflection. Carson notes that confidence in a coherent canon extends beyond a mere historical process of canonization in the early stages of church history, but moves on to a coherence derived from something intrinsic in the texts themselves. This suggests a rather developed notion of revelation that is necessary in pursuing BT2.

Third, biblical theology must exhibit a *"profound willingness to work inductively from the text—from individual books and from the canon as a whole."*[21] Here again we see Carson's concern to mark up the line between biblical theology and systematic theology clearly. The characteristic of working "inductively from the text" is a distinctive of biblical theology that is not, in Carson's understanding, true of systematic theology. Whereas systematic theology attends to "atemporal questions" resulting in a second or third level remove from the text, biblical theology's focus is set by the text itself. He carefully nuances this point:

---

17. Carson, "Current Issues," 27 (emphasis original).
18. George E. Ladd, *The Pattern of New Testament Truth* (Grand Rapids: Eerdmans, 1968), 10–11; noted in Carson "Current Issues," 27 n.46.
19. Carson, "Systematic Theology and Biblical Theology," 90.
20. Carson, "Current Issues," 27 (emphasis original).
21. Carson, "Current Issues," 29 (emphasis original).

> This is not of course to suggest that any biblical theologian can ever escape his or her limitations, self-identity, place in culture and history.... But a biblical theologian, whether working on, say, the Pauline corpus, or on the entire canon, must in the first instance seek to deploy categories and pursue an agenda set by the text itself.[22]

Even with this careful qualification, however, Carson does not elaborate on precisely how the text is able to set the agenda for biblical theology, while failing to do so for systematic theology. We will discuss this critique in more detail in the assessment section.

Fourth, working inductively from the biblical material, biblical theology must also "*seek to make clear the connections among the* [biblical] *corpora.*" Of course this extends beyond just the intertextual relationships between historically related documents. Carson notes that biblical theology in its most coherent and unified moment "is a theology of the *Bible*."[23] Here "ideally, biblical theology will not only work inductively in each of the biblical corpora, but will seek to make clear the connections among the corpora."[24] As noted in the previous chapter, this is where Carson and the Chicago school move beyond the Dallas school; rather than a biblical theology limited to the theology of Matthew or Isaiah, "ideally" biblical theology extends beyond individual books or collections of books to consider the connections throughout the entire canon. Thus Carson is fond of referring to a "whole-Bible" biblical theology.

Finally, Carson argues for the prescriptive function of a proper biblical theology: "*biblical theology will transcend mere description ... and call men and women to knowledge of the living God.*" Rather than a mere intellectual exercise, a fully "useful" biblical theology practically calls individuals to a new way of living—it calls hearers to repentance and transformation. It must, in Carson's words, "call a new generation to personal knowledge of the living God."[25] This characteristic of BT2 stands in clear contrast to BT1, where what ancient people believed about God fails to exert any necessary influence on modern readers.

A BIBLICAL THEOLOGY FOR THE CHURCH

Moving from the conviction that biblical theology must serve the prescriptive task of calling individuals to faith, Carson unequivocally argues that from the Christian perspective, "disciplined biblical exegesis and thoughtful

---

22. Ibid.
23. Ibid., 30 (emphasis original).
24. Ibid., 31.
25. Ibid.

systematic theology do not exist for themselves. They exist, finally, to serve the people of God." He insists the "message that is distilled out of such work must be preachable and preached, or ... the entire exercise is such a distortion of the *purposes* of revelation as to approach profanity."[26] Because biblical theology, for Carson, is the bridge between exegesis and systematic theology, biblical theology is central to the task of directing exegesis to systematic theology for the ultimate purpose of preaching God's Word. In short, biblical theology is indispensible for both the preacher and the academic. Carson continues:

> But there is a sense in which the best expository preaching ought also to be the best exemplification of the relationship between biblical exegesis and systematic theology.... As a general rule, the best expository preaching begins with the text at hand but seeks to establish links not only to the immediate context but also to the canonical context, *as determined by the biblico-theological constraints largely governed by the canon itself.* If these lines are sketched out in the course of regular, expository ministry, believers begin to see how their Bibles cohere.[27]

Discovering the "links" within the text "*as determined by the biblico-theological constraints*" is clearly the task of biblical theology. Carson is advocating the necessity of biblical theology not only in the task of biblical interpretation, but also for the task of preaching and the spiritual formation of Christians as well.

Along with understanding how "their Bibles cohere," biblical theology directs one's preaching such that hearers see Christ in all Scripture. Carson notes his "enormous sympathy with efforts to preach Christ from all the Scriptures." However, he cautions that "the most responsible of such efforts ... depend on the legitimacy of complex (and textually authenticated) typologies ... rather than on a kind of homiletical fiat that simply declares a particular passage is talking explicitly about Jesus."[28] As we briefly consider below, Carson understands the unity of Scripture as demonstrated by means of typological connections. Typology supports the academic task of biblical theology; yet here Carson also articulates the role of typology in legitimately "preaching of Christ from all the Scriptures." He concludes,

---

26. Carson, "Exegesis in Systematic Theology," 70–71 (emphasis original).

27. Ibid., 71 (emphasis original).

28. D. A. Carson, "Biblical-Theological Ruminations of Psalm 1," in *Resurrection and Eschatology: Theology in Service of the Church: Essays in Honor of Richard B. Gaffin Jr.* (ed. Lane G. Tipton and Jeffery C. Waddington; Phillipsburg, NJ: Presbyterian & Reformed, 2008), 125.

"Christian readers are right to look for clear textual markers before they affirm such connections in such straightforward claims about the psalm's [Ps. 1] referents."[29]

Again, Naselli summarizes this notion by arguing:

> ...the pressing need in contemporary evangelism to postmoderns is to "start further back and nail down the turning points in redemptive history," give primacy to BT rather than ST, herald "the rudiments of the historic gospel," and "think through what to say" and "how to live".... BT is primary because the gospel "is virtually incoherent unless it is securely set into a biblical worldview."[30]

CONTINUITY AND THE PROBLEM OF THE CONNECTION BETWEEN THE TESTAMENTS

Carson is clearly concerned for how the Old and New Testaments fit together. As we noted in the previous chapter, BT2 understands the connection between the Testaments as founded primarily on the two hermeneutical claims that Scripture is both God's progressive revelation and, as God's Word, a progressive unity. Carson argues that biblical theology seeks to "uncover and articulate the unity of all the biblical texts taken together resorting primarily to the categories of those texts themselves."[31] Inductively, one aspect of this unity can be demonstrated in "the categories of those texts themselves" by the NT's use of the OT.

For Carson, the gospel of Matthew and the letter to the Hebrews offer inductive examples of how the two Testaments interact with each other and thus the character and kind of unity existing between them. The key theme connecting the Old and New Testaments that surfaces not only in Matthew and Hebrews, but also throughout the entire NT, is the use of typology. Biblical typology, for this discussion, is a historical correspondence or pattern established between two events or stages in the fulfillment of God's purposes in history.[32] And for Carson, typology is one of the primary methods by

---

29. Ibid.
30. Naselli, "Carson's Theological Method," 269–70.
31. Carson, "Systematic Theology and Biblical Theology," 100.
32. For example: Israel's entry and possession of the land as a type of the Christian's entering into God's promised rest through faith; Israel's priesthood and sacrificial system as a type of Christ's ultimate priesthood and sacrifice; or Israel's captivity and release in the exodus as a type of Christian captivity to sin brought to an end by Christ's death. See Graeme Goldsworthy, *Gospel-Centered Hermeneutics: Foundations and Principles of Evangelical Biblical Interpretation* (Downers Grove, IL: InterVarsity Press, 2006), 253–57.

which the unity and progression of the Bible finds articulation.[33] Whether in preaching or in academic argument, biblical theology helps an interpreter avoid unjustified and speculative associations between the Testaments by working toward warranted interconnections by means of typological fulfillment. Thus typology serves as evidence of genuine connection between Old and New Testaments, but it also serves as a key hermeneutical tool in Carson's notion of biblical theology.

THE SCOPE OF BIBLICAL THEOLOGY IN CARSON'S WORK

Carson explicitly states that biblical theology is "bounded" in two particular ways: "First, its subject matter is exclusively biblical. At root, it is the result of the inductive study of the text of Scripture."[34] So, obviously, the subject matter for biblical theology is the Christian Scriptures—the Old and New Testaments. But here he also articulates how one should read these texts. The Christian Scriptures must be interpreted from the inside out—that is inductively. Though for some this might sound hopelessly simplistic, as we saw above, Carson is not naïve to the interpreter's theological convictions that doubtlessly shape one's exegetical conclusions.

Carson's second boundary is that biblical theology

> organizes its subject matter in ways that preserve corpus distinctions. It is less interested in what the New Testament or the Bible says about, say, the sovereignty of God, than it is in what Paul (or Isaiah, or John) says about this subject. When such distinctions are observed, then biblical theology may be interested in probing common points or differences in perspective among the biblical corpora, but the distinctions themselves are never lost to view.[35]

Here we discover a key way in which biblical theology is limited. When considering the degree of unity within the diversity of Scripture, biblical theology, for Carson, attempts to hold on to the tension—stressing conceptual

---

33. Perhaps typology stands as a key difference between Dallas and Chicago. Whereas Dallas is concerned with whole-Bible synthesis at the level of systematic theology, such overarching connections must be made historically and grammatically. Chicago is much more open to typology as it pursues such synthesis. Typology also plays a key role in BT5. For BT5 typology not only provides genuine connections between OT and NT moving forward, but also provides connections from NT to OT moving backwards. Thus, for BT5, typology allows for a forward and backward movement that highlights the *dianoia* ("mind") of Scripture. On this point see chapter 2 in Peter J. Leithart, *Deep Exegesis: The Mystery of Reading Scripture* (Waco, TX: Baylor University Press, 2009).

34. Carson, "Exegesis in Systematic Theology," 45.

35. Ibid.

unity without erasing the variety and complexity of the particular texts themselves. Above we noted that Carson moves beyond the Dallas school by insisting biblical theology (not just systematic theology) must "*seek to make clear the connections among the* [biblical] *corpora.*" Yet, by claiming that biblical theology "is less interested in what the New Testament or the Bible says about, say, the sovereignty of God, than it is in what Paul (or Isaiah, or John) says about this subject," Carson holds back from the Philadelphia school. Further, because biblical theology keeps these differences in view, Carson notes, "This means, in turn, that biblical theology is organized chronologically, or, better, salvation-historically (another admittedly slippery term!)—both within any one corpus (e.g., What development is there in Paul?) and from corpus to corpus."[36]

As described in the previous chapter, Carson notes in the preface to New Studies in Biblical Theology:

> Contributions to the series focus on one or more of three areas: 1. The nature and status of biblical theology ...; 2. The articulation and exposition of the structure of thought of a particular biblical writer or corpus; and 3. The delineation of a biblical theme across all or part of the biblical corpora.

He seems to move beyond the Dallas school with criterion 3, but resists the more aggressive synthesis of Philadelphia in criterion 2. Here again the distinction between biblical theology and systematic theology surfaces—biblical theology cannot synthesize to the point systematic theology can because biblical theology is bound by chronological development and must keep distinctions among the biblical corpora in view.

ASSESSMENT

Carson is well known for his careful and exacting exegesis accompanied with a clear and unadorned expression. Though he has not written on the methodology of biblical theology per se, he might have provided something much more useful in getting on with the task and doing work characterized

---

36. Ibid. In the same passage, Carson defines systematic theology as "Christian theology whose internal structure is systematic; i.e., it is organized on atemporal principles of logic, order, and need, rather than on inductive study of discrete biblical corpora. Thus it can address the broader concerns of Christian theology (it is not merely inductive study of the Bible, though it must never lose such controls), but it seeks to be rigorously systematic and is therefore concerned about how various parts of God's gracious self-disclosure cohere" (ibid, 45). But even here Carson provides some helpful nuance, for on p. 46 he says: "By saying that systematic theology is organized on 'atemporal principles' I mean that the questions it poses are atemporal—not that the questioner occupies a spot outside time, but that the focal concerns are logical and hierarchical, not salvation-historical."

by a rich understanding of biblical theology. His abundant contributions to biblical interpretation will remain valuable to those interested in careful and exegetically rich work. A clear strength of Carson's work is that while demonstrating an unusual ability to see the details of Scripture clearly, he is concerned to set such careful analysis within the overarching picture of Scripture.

Articulating one of the formal challenges to biblical theology as a discipline, Carson expresses the *"need for exegetes and theologians who will deploy the full range of weapons in the exegetical arsenal, without succumbing to methodological narrowness or faddishness."*[37] He elaborates by warning against the particular narrowness promoted by the minutiae of grammatical exegesis, which in its more myopic moments cannot focus on literary genre let alone larger themes of biblical theology. Carson not only sounds a clarion call for the importance of biblical theology, but he himself has filled shelves with works that reach beyond such narrowness.

While noting the clear value of Carson's works, here we offer an appreciative critique. As noted above, though Carson nuances the linear development of the "exegesis–biblical theology–[historical theology]–systematic theology" progression, he unequivocally asserts that "the line of final control is the straight one from exegesis right through biblical and historical theology to systematic theology." Thus, biblical theology functions as a "bridge discipline," providing the necessary step between exegesis and systematic theology. This view of biblical theology seems to suggest that (1) there are forms of exegesis that are not influenced by biblical theology, and (2) there are forms of systematic theology not nourished by biblical theology. Directly to this point Richard Gaffin notes: "Exegesis itself is misunderstood if biblical theology is seen as no more than a step (even the most important) in the exegetical process." Rather than implicitly allowing for exegesis as a starting point all on its own, Gaffin continues: "All exegesis ought to be biblical-theological. To the extent that there is hesitation on this point the relationship between biblical and systematic theology will remain unresolved."[38]

Gaffin's comment surfaces another point of critique, namely, Carson's insistence on the discontinuity between biblical theology and systematic theology rather than their continuity. Carson acknowledges that both biblical theology and systematic theology distort or abstract the text of Scripture. This need not be a negative acknowledgment or a concession because such abstraction is necessary. Just as a map of Yosemite National Park distorts the

---

37. Carson, "Current Issues," 34.
38. Gaffin, "Systematic and Biblical Theology," 294.

actual valley (the map is not to scale), it is fantastically helpful to find one's way to a particular trailhead (let alone, manage to reach Half Dome). Thus, abstracting from the text of Scripture is not necessarily the problem. Rather, it is Carson's claim that systematic theology, by definition, is at a further remove from the text.

With respect to the distortion caused by both biblical theology and systematic theology, Carson claims:

> To a lesser degree, the same is doubtless true of biblical theology; it easily distorts the very texts it seeks to explicate. But it is intrinsically less distorting, because methodologically it stands closer to the text than systematic theology, aims to achieve genuine sensitivity with respect to the distinctiveness of each corpus, and seeks to connect the diverse corpora using their own categories.[39]

Thus biblical theology is closer to the text because it is sensitive to the distinctiveness of each biblical corpus and works with the text's own categories. Systematic theology, by contrast, stands further from the text because of its engagement with the atemporalities of reason and philosophy. Whereas reason and philosophy are tools of abstraction, they are necessary for understanding. Though perhaps in a different category, history too is an instrument of abstraction to the same degree as reason and philosophy. Rather than extracting timeless principles that can be transported from the text, history, as an abstracting tool, can reconfigure the narrative shape of Scripture into sequential development. Carson (and BT2 in general) seems to underplay the abstracting character of history alongside that of reason and philosophy. History is not as neutral as Carson's implicit construction suggests.

---

39. Carson, "Systematic Theology and Biblical Theology," 94.

Part 3

TYPE 3: BIBLICAL THEOLOGY AS WORLDVIEW-STORY

Chapter 5

BIBLICAL THEOLOGY AS WORLDVIEW-STORY: DEFINITION

The third type of biblical theology (BT3) attempts to balance historical and theological concerns through the category of narrative. Rather than emphasizing connections between successive events in the one, continuous redemption history (BT2) or relying on purely descriptive historical development (BT1) to discern unity, a Biblical Theology as Worldview-Story affirms the overarching "story shape" or narrative connection between the Old and New Testaments as constitutive of the Bible's theology. Read as a continuous and interconnected narrative—especially paying close attention to how earlier narrative episodes are understood, interpreted, and taken up in later parts of the story—this perspective discerns a narrative continuity running throughout the whole Bible.

Many working with this narrative structure of the Bible's unity would not consider this approach as "biblical theology" per se; rather, the concerns that shape this type of reading originate from a desire to read Scripture without historical criticism functioning as the primary methodology. Positively, BT3 argues that the theological shape of Scripture surfaces by focusing on the narrative aspect of Paul's (or the NT's) use of Israel's "story." Again, rather than starting with questions of historical development (BT1) or the necessity of a progressive historical development of God's purposes (BT2), BT3 assumes a narrative unity as *the* starting point for reading the Bible as a whole.

While refusing to prioritize historical-critical methodology, BT3 does attempt to balance literary concerns with historical concerns. This task is accomplished primarily through a rich description of the literary intertextuality, especially that found in the NT's use of the OT. For many working within BT3 this rich, intertextual reading of Scripture, in turn, offers a prescription for living as a disciple of Jesus Christ. Yet just here we see something of the flexibility of BT3. From the start we can discern two trajectories within this emphasis on narrative. Some working within a narrative approach to biblical theology focus on reconstructing the *historical* world of the author and audience, which then informs the overarching narrative unity of the Bible. Others focus on the *literary* coherence of the narrative with much less concern for how that narrative refers to events of history outside the text itself.

Both of these trajectories use the category of narrative to balance literary, historical, and theological elements in the text. Whereas BT2 is interested in a similar balance, BT2 leans toward the history end of the spectrum, resting the task of biblical theology on the foundational claim that Scripture is a historically unfolding progression. BT3, by comparison, begins from the claim that the Bible's unity is fundamentally a quality of its narrative structure or "story" shape. Thus, BT3 works to understand the interconnections between the Testaments through the lens of narrative and to discern the theological world that flows out of this coherent "story-shaped" reading of the Bible with varying degrees of reference to the historical events behind the text of Scripture.

THE TASK OF BIBLICAL THEOLOGY

The stress on reading the Bible in light of its narrative unity is not new. Long before there was an academic discipline of biblical studies or the modern notion of biblical theology, students of Scripture implicitly knew that the entire Bible should be read as a complete and coherent whole. Especially supported by the notion that God himself has revealed his vantage point on history in the text, many understood the Bible as a narrative whole told from one, divine perspective. For example, Irenaeus viewed Scripture as a single narrative where the central perspective and actor was God himself.[1]

For Augustine the internal coherence of Scripture functioned as a basic

---

1. Irenaeus argues: "Two histories converge in the biblical account, the history of Israel and the life of Christ, but because they are also the history of God's actions in and for the world, they are part of a larger narrative that begins at creation and ends in a vision of a new, more splendid city in which the 'Lord God will be their light'" (as quoted in Craig G. Bartholomew, "Introduction," in *Out of Egypt: Biblical Theology and Biblical Interpretation* [ed. Craig Bartholomew et al.; SHS 5; Grand Rapids: Zondervan, 2004], 3).

hermeneutic: "after gaining a familiarity with the language of the divine scriptures, one should proceed to explore and analyse the obscure passages, by taking examples from the more obvious parts to illuminate obscure expressions" (*On Christian Teaching* 3.31).

Calvin's redemptive-historical approach also works with the understanding of the Bible as an unfolding story (*Institutes* 2.10 – 11), a perspective that Jonathan Edwards picks up and explains analytically.[2] Though biblical theology as "narrative" shares characteristics in common with these historical figures, their approaches must be distinguished from the contemporary focus on literature and narrative.[3]

Rather than founded primarily on the theological conviction that God himself is the author of Scripture, which renders it a complete narrative whole, much of the post-Enlightenment concern with the overall literary shape of the Bible has been prompted by the concerns of narrative theology and related literary-centered readings of the text. Stated succinctly, *using the category of narrative to broker a balance between history and theology, the task of BT3 directs readers to understand the individual episodes or passages of Scripture in light of its overarching story line. Instead of progressing from the smallest bits and pieces of the narrative to the larger whole, BT3 starts with the larger narrative portions of text through which individual units are read.* This can be supported by several necessary explanations.

First, for BT3 narrative is both a literary as well as a philosophical category. The modern importance of narrative has been noted beyond the disciplines of theology or biblical studies. Philosophers such as Paul Ricoeur and Alasdair MacIntyre have reconceived literature, history, and ethics in terms of narrative. Ricoeur observes that history in particular and the way humans live in the world are implicitly narratival. That is to say, knowledge of ourselves and the world around us is inescapably cast in a narrative shape. He argues the narrative form of history is not just mere packaging; it is a form of understanding, what Ricoeur calls "explanation by emplotment."[4] In the

---

2. Jonathan Edwards, *A History of the Work of Redemption* (The Works of Jonathan Edwards, vol. 9; New Haven, CT: Yale Univ. Press, 1989).

3. Some modern concerns to read Scripture in light of its narrative unity do continue this conviction. A group of scholars participating in the Scripture Project at the Center of Theological Inquiry in Princeton argue this point in the edited volume *The Art of Reading Scripture* (ed. Ellen F. Davis and Richard B. Hays; Grand Rapids: Eerdmans, 2003). Speaking for this group, Hays argues that the "unity of the Bible is grounded in the ongoing action of the one God who is both its central character and its ultimate author. Because God is one, Scripture turns out to be coherent" (Richard B. Hays, "Can Narrative Criticism Recover the Theological Unity of Scripture?," *JTI* 2 (2008): 202.

4. Paul Ricoeur, *Time and Narrative* (Chicago: Univ. of Chicago Press, 1990), 1:181; see also 1:257 n. 54.

realm of ethics, MacIntyre famously notes: "I can only answer the question, 'What am I to do?' if I can answer the prior question, 'Of what story do I find myself a part?'"[5]

Second, the particular application of narrative as a category for biblical theology surfaces from an explicit critique of historical criticism. The move toward narrative theology and literary-centered readings of Scripture take their modern starting point in Hans Frei's now famous critique of historical criticism in *The Eclipse of Biblical Narrative.*[6] The historical-critical approach to interpretation revolves around reconstructing the historical and sociological background of the text, which in turn offers assured results in clear, historical understanding—an approach strongly influential for both BT1 and BT2. For Frei, the historical-critical approach, through fragmentation and technical minutiae, loses sight of the larger narrative connections running through and connecting the overarching plotline of the Bible. And this, especially for critics of BT1, results in relegating the Bible to the past and, consequently, distances the text from the modern reader.

Against such historical reductionism, Frei argued that the historical-critical insistence on reading the text merely to discover its referent (that is, how the Bible refers to historical events behind the text), rather than reading the text as a coherent narrative itself, has led to great distortion and misunderstanding of the central subject matter of the Bible. Frei's concerns are relevant for BT3, BT4, and BT5, with each of these types of biblical theology making particular use of his insights. Frei's importance for BT3 surfaces in his observation that the central subject matter of the Bible does not come into focus through the historical or social context *behind* the text, but only through the story line running *through* the text.

Third, because the story line running *through* the text is *the* key to the Bible's subject matter, the narrative approach relies on the plotline of the Bible's story as a means to understand each individual passage. Because the Bible is a unified and interconnected story, the purposeful forward movement of events, or plotline,[7] serves as a key to discerning how individual episodes or passages find their place within the whole. Working within a narrative framework, John Goldingay argues that "a key aspect of [biblical narratives'] theological

---

5. Alasdair MacIntyre, *After Virtue: A Study in Moral Theory* (Notre Dame, IN: Notre Dame Press, 1984), 216.

6. Hans W. Frei, *The Eclipse of Biblical Narrative: Studies in Eighteenth and Ninteenth Century Hermeneutics* (New Haven, CT: Yale Univ. Press, 1974).

7. See Peter Brooks, *Reading for the Plot: Design and Intention in Narrative* (Oxford: Clarendon, 1984), 5, notes: "Plot is the principle of interconnectedness and intention which we cannot do without in moving through the discrete elements-incidents, episodes, actions—of a narrative."

significance will be conveyed by their plot."[8] Interpretation that takes into account how each author narrates a sequence of actions by emplotting them will begin to shed light on the larger story shape of Scripture. Thus "plot" and "story" are related—plot is the discrete sequence of interconnected action as depicted by an individual author, where story is the overarching shape of reality. An author puts down a plot in his narration of events as he looks at the story in his mind's eye.

Finally, narrative not only stresses the interconnections within the text, but also how this unified narrative is relevant for modern readers. The rise of historical criticism drastically emphasized the distance separating the modern reader from the Bible itself. In the face of such a development, Craig Bartholomew and Michael Goheen understand Scripture as "a unified and progressively unfolding drama of God's action in history for the salvation of the whole world."[9] Highlighting the implications for modern readers, Bartholomew and Goheen argue elsewhere that a "narrative biblical theology can play a role in making the church—including biblical scholars—aware of the grand story that *ought to be shaping their whole lives*."[10]

N. T. Wright has artfully argued for the dramatic understanding of both the Bible's narrative unity and of how a "story" might be authoritative for readers today.[11] He argues that such a reading of Scripture aids the church in faithfully living out God's kingdom commands. Using the analogy of individual acts in a play, Wright suggests living out the story line of Scripture as an actor reads and enacts the script of a play. After arguing that the "authority of scripture" must be understood as God's authority rendered through the overarching story line, he notes: "'the authority of scripture' is most truly put into operation as the church goes to work in the world on behalf of the gospel, the good news that in Jesus Christ the living God has defeated the powers of evil and begun the work of new creation." Because "the New Testament

---

8. John Goldingay, "Biblical Narrative and Systematic Theology," in *Between Two Horizons: Spanning New Testament Studies and Systematic Theology* (ed. Joel B. Green and Max Turner; Grand Rapids: Eerdmans, 2000), 125.

9. Craig Bartholomew and Michael Goheen, *The Drama of Scripture: Finding Our Place in the Biblical Story* (Grand Rapids: Baker, 2004), 12. Bartholomew and Goheen have suggested that the kingdom or reign of God is the most helpful overall thread that can be traced through all of the Scripture's story.

10. Craig G. Bartholomew and Mike W. Goheen, "Story and Biblical Theology," in *Out of Egypt*, 158 (emphasis added).

11. See N. T. Wright's *New Testament and the People of God* (London: SPCK, 1992) and *Scripture and the Authority of God* (London: SPCK, 2005). Several have suggested thinking about the "story of Scripture" as a drama with several distinct acts. Kevin Vanhoozer develops an entire way of understanding the doctrinal content and direction of Christian Scripture in his thought-provoking, if not massive, *The Drama of Doctrine* (Louisville: Westminster/John Knox, 2005).

offers us glimpses of where the story is to end," Wright concludes, this gives readers reference to how to live now, not expecting the annihilation of the world "but new creation."[12]

THE USE OF BIBLICAL THEOLOGY

Who is able to "do" this kind of biblical theology and to what use might BT3 be put? If the task of biblical theology for BT3 is to broker a balance between history and theology using the category of narrative, the natural question arises as to who is competent to master each of these concerns that themselves constitute stand-alone disciplines. While its historical approach to the biblical narrative is dependent on the work of the academy, the guidance provided by the resources of theology speaks directly to the church.

Though reading Scripture as a coherent and interconnected story has been the default position for much of the church's history — at least from Irenaeus (if not Paul) to Edwards — the modern emphasis on narrative as both a literary and philosophical category rests heavily on the academy's contribution. The technical tools and well-groomed theory of narrative and intertextuality requires the resources and methodological precision that usually only a university context can provide. Nevertheless, a significant motivation for reading the Bible as a coherent story comes from a Christian desire to live richly into the "strange new world" of the Bible.

This raises the question of who actually is able to do BT3. Is this a task of the pastor in the local church? Is it something only a scholar with the intellectual resources of the university can accomplish? Though the skilled pastor might strive for a holistic reading of Scripture, after considering the complexity of such reading below, the church leader might despair of ever reproducing their readings of biblical theology.

The complexity of BT3, like any story, has numerous versions. But this approach to biblical theology offers a thick, intertextual reading of the whole Bible that serves to coalesce the diverse parts of the Bible with the whole, as well as the story of God with the story of its readers. Biblical Theology as Worldview-Story is constructed and maintained directly between the academy's narrative tools and the church's living script that is already being enacted and lived out. Often the union is better in theory than in practice. For some the academy is the primary constructing agent, for others the church's contemporary story and practice. Ultimately both are required to play their part.

---

12. Wright, *Scripture and the Authority of God*, 85, 93.

THE SCOPE AND SOURCES OF BIBLICAL THEOLOGY

Since BT3's central concern is to balance history and theology via the overall narrative shape of the Bible, its scope and sources might seem clear. The sources for BT3 are the canonical texts of the Old and New Testaments with the scope necessarily including the narrative range of all those texts—from Genesis to Revelation. In general, then, a narrative approach to biblical theology will pay special attention to how the canonical texts of the Old and New Testaments flow together in one fluid and interconnected direction. Yet beyond this general conviction are various ways of describing the particular shape of this narrative unity. Narrative attempts to discern unity in the story line of Scripture aggregate toward one of two centers.

First, it is common for those working with the narrative interconnections of the Bible to focus on how the NT's use of the OT serves as a key for discerning overall unity. Several scholars[13] have discerned the narrative continuity of the Bible as they study Paul's reading of Israel's Scriptures. The Bible's narrative unity surfaces especially as Paul or Jesus interpret the OT and find an underlying story line running through and between the OT passages they cite. This approach and others like it tend to limit the range of sources for discerning narrative biblical theology. Rather than attending to each of the canonical texts equally, this approach looks particularly to those OT texts that are taken up in the NT as a means to discern the Bible's narrative unity.

Second, with other narrative strategies, the sources extend beyond the canonical texts, allowing extracanonical sources to inform the coherence of the biblical narrative. A distinction between "narrative" and "story"[14] will help clarify the following discussion. "Story" often refers to the sequence of events that the author of the text takes for granted—that is, events that the author assumes represent reality. "Narrative," by contrast, refers to the author's representation of that "story" in a particular text. To discover this "story" (sequence of events) one must pay careful attention to just how the author composes the "narrative."

One form of narrative analysis, for example, is to rearrange the implicit references to the "story" in the "narrative" (whether they are in or out of order in the "narrative") so that the "story" becomes clear. Note that this "story"

---

13. See the variety of scholarly voices, for example, in Bruce Longenecker, ed. *Narrative Dynamics in Paul: A Critical Assessment* (Louisville: Westminster/John Knox, 2002), and Longenecker's excellent summary in "The Narrative Approach to Paul: An Early Retrospective," *CurBR* 1 (2002): 88–111.
14. Gérard Genette, *Narrative Discourse Revisited* (trans. Jane E. Lewin; Ithaca, NY: Cornell Univ. Press, 1988), 13.

might assume the sequence of events of the OT (which a majority of the time it does), but it could plausibly include events from Israel's history not included in the OT proper. That is, some of the "story" events come not only from the OT "story" but also from the Second Temple "story" found in extracanonical sources such as *1 Enoch*. Thus, in this version of BT3 extracanonical sources may surface as part of the underlying narrative coherence within which the Bible itself must be understood.

N. T. Wright's version of BT3 is a clear example of openness to extracanonical sources. As we will demonstrate in much more detail in the next chapter, Wright's method focuses on a historical reconstruction of the worldview of the biblical authors themselves, which in turn produces the narrative shape or "story-world" of the NT. By way of summary, BT3 seeks to discern the overall narrative coherence running through the Old and New Testaments, but as this short section indicates, the sources for such an argument vary from strictly canonical to the inclusion of extracanonical sources, depending on one's methodology.

THE HERMENEUTICAL APPROACH OF BIBLICAL THEOLOGY

The hermeneutical approach of BT3 centers on the task of reading every passage, whether small or large, within the context of the overarching story shape of Scripture—understanding the parts in light of the coherent whole. Within BT3 there are a few perspectives on exactly how to understand the overall story shape of Scripture. For example, one could focus on the historical realities that shape the worldview born out in the text. That is, rather than a single theme disclosed through progressive revelation, this perspective seeks to reconstruct the historically grounded worldview of the biblical authors, which, in turn, shapes the story structure of Scripture ("worldview-story" with both elements taken together, a neologism invented by N. T. Wright). Wright will serve as an exceptionally good example of this kind of narrative biblical theology (see next chapter).

Yet another way to discover the overarching coherence of Scripture is to rely heavily on how NT authors use the OT. This largely intertextual move understands the interconnected narrative of Scripture as taking shape specifically through either Paul's or Jesus' interpretation of the OT. Richard Hays serves as a clear example of this type of approach. For Hays, Paul has discovered a new theological reality by noting how the reality of Jesus Christ casts its shadow across the story line of the OT. The key tool for Hays to discover Paul's new reading of Israel's Scripture through the reality of Jesus is the phenomenon of literary intertextuality. His specific concern is to gain access to the narrative unity between the Old and New Testaments through the interpretive practices of Paul himself. Often the unintended consequences of this approach are that (1) OT texts not taken up in the NT are deemphasized, and (2) OT texts that are mentioned in the NT are usually read *only* as the NT understands them.[15]

However one discovers the overarching coherence of the Bible, it is this narrative coherence or overarching story that serves as the hermeneutical lens through which individual passages or books find their theological significance. Hermeneutically the distinction between "story" and "narrative" serves as a key element of BT3. In an excellent essay, "Reading Scripture as a Coherent Story," Richard Bauckham notes well the significance of this narrative distinction:

> At this point it may be helpful to remember the distinction that the narratologist Gérard Genette makes between story and narrative. A literary narrative may differ in many ways from the story it tells (regardless of whether the story is construed as fictional or true). For example, the order in which the events are narrated may differ from the order in which they occur in the story. A narrative need not tell all the events of the story, while it may recount some events a number of times — from different points of view (whether of characters or narrators), from different temporal junctures within the story, conveying different information, highlighting different aspects of significance. This important distinction between story and narrative may help us to see that the plurality of narratives in Scripture … is not in principle an obstacle to seeking in the Bible a single coherent story, which all the narratives together tell and each partially tells.[16]

---

15. See Christopher R. Seitz, *The Character of Christian Scripture: The Significance of a Two-Testament Bible* (STI; Grand Rapids: Baker, 2011). Referring specifically to Hays's method of constructing biblical theology on the foundation of Paul's reading of the OT, Seitz notes: "The problem is that, in the realm of biblical theology of the Christian Scriptures as a twofold witness, the OT threatens to be swallowed up into Paul's confessions and construals about it…. [Hays's] narrative world is an abstraction derived by recourse to historical tools, and it exists apart from the canonical form of the Pauline Letter collection and the influence this form has on interpretation" (84). This critique represents a major fault line running between BT3 and BT4. Seitz, clearly working within a BT4 framework, is concerned that the whole of the Christian canon, both Old and New Testaments, be heard as Christian Scripture. Though making a rather different point, Goldingay's comments are relevant here: "The agenda for Old Testament theology is set by the Old Testament as a whole and the agenda for biblical theology is set by the Scriptures as a whole, not just those parts of them that especially link with the New" (*Old Testament Theology* [Downers Grove, IL: InterVarsity Press, 2003], 1:25).

16. Richard Bauckham, "Reading Scripture as a Coherent Story," in Davis and Hays, eds., *The Art of Reading Scripture*, 43.

Bauckham's insight clarifies the key relationship between "story" and "narrative." While the sequence of real or imagined events (the "story") constitutes the subject matter of the author's writing ("narrative"), interpreters must be careful to note just how the author chooses to rendor the narrative and how such a telling reveals the significance of the story being told.

There are a variety of ways scholars make this key hermeneutical move from narrative to story in their work. Focusing on the implicit story in the letters of Paul, Richard Hays draws three conclusions:

> (1) There can be an organic relationship between stories and reflective discourse [specifically the non-narrative, didactic material in Paul's letters] because stories have an inherent configurational dimension (*dianoia*) which not only permits but also demands restatement and interpretation in non-narrative language.
>
> (2) The reflective restatement does not simply repeat the plot (*mythos*) of the story: nonetheless, the story shapes and constrains the reflective process because the *dianoia* can never be entirely abstracted from the story in which it is manifested and apprehended.
>
> (3) Hence, when we encounter this type of reflective discourse, it is legitimate and possible to inquire about the story in which it is rooted.[17]

Hays notes the important connection between Paul's composition (his "narrative") and the implicit story it assumes. He argues that "we may first identify within [Paul's letters] allusions to the story and seek to discern its general outlines; then, in a second phase of inquiry we must ask how this story shapes the logic of argumentation of [his letters]."[18] Here we can see Hays's strategy for reading Scripture; as he looks over Paul's shoulder, he sees how Paul himself reads and interprets Israel's Scriptures. In composing his letter to the Galatians, for example, Paul reflects back on the overarching shape and direction of the OT, which becomes the framework ("narrative substructure") for Paul's understanding of the significance of Jesus Christ. Hays continues: "If there are 'constant elements of the gospel' for Paul, they are to be sought in the structure of this story."[19] For Hays, the "story" found in the OT becomes the framework over which Paul stretches out the narrative fabric of his gospel.

Working with similar tools in studying Paul, Ben Witherington describes the contours of Paul's theology as "Paul's narrative thought world." He argues

---

17. Richard B. Hays, *The Faith of Jesus Christ: An Investigation of the Narrative Substructure of Galatians 3:1–4:11* (Chico, CA: Scholars, 1983), 28.
18. Ibid., 28.
19. Ibid., 6.

for the "fundamental Story out of which all his discourses arise."[20] Displaying the key characteristics of BT3, Witherington understands that the story of Scripture (or at least the story of the OT) lies just underneath or prior to Paul's composition. Witherington summarizes key elements in his understanding of how Paul's "narrative" (again, his composition) relates to the "story":

> (1) Paul's symbolic universe, which entails those things that Paul takes to be inherently true and real, the fixed stars in Paul's mental sky; (2) Paul's narrative thought world, which is Paul's reflections on his symbolic universe in terms of the grand Story. This undergirds (3) Paul's articulation of his theology, ethics and so forth, in response to the situations he must address.[21]

Though Witherington does not use the terms story and narrative with the same kind of precision as Hays, we see a similar narrative move. Paul's theology and ethics flow out of the "grand Story" that gives shape to his writings.

Registering a broader concern for a narrative theology of the OT, John Goldingay serves as a third example. Though Goldingay does not work so tightly within the hermeneutical distinction between story and narrative and whereas his analysis focuses primarily on the OT, his concern for the narrative connections running through the whole of Scripture place him in the BT3 segment of our spectrum. Goldingay notes the frequency of narrative texts in the OT, yet argues, "more important than the shaping of individual books or their order is the rhetorical form of the canon. It is indeed dominated by narrative." He continues: "The canon's being dominated by narrative signifies for Old Testament theology that Israel's faith is a gospel, a story declaring good news about what God has done."[22]

For Goldingay the good news of the OT, which points to Jesus Christ, is revealed through the overarching story of God's relationship with Israel. "These narratives," he notes, "are not just one collection of liberating stories and traditions, parallel to other such collections from other cultures. They tell us *the* good news about what God did for Israel in setting about to bless the world. And their narrative form is intrinsic to their theological statement."[23] Yet just here Goldingay demonstrates his nuanced view of narrative, for rather than narrative only supporting the theological message of the OT, it is at the same time historical. "An Old Testament narrative theology is dependent on the factuality of the events it refers to." He continues:

---

20. Ben Witherington, *Paul's Narrative Thought World* (Louisville: Westminster/John Knox, 1994), 2.
21. Ibid., 6 n.7.
22. John Goldingay, "Old Testament Theology and the Canon," *TynBul* 59 (2008): 4.
23. Ibid., 4–5 (emphasis original).

The basic historicity of the Old Testament story is important to the validity of its theology. (I do not know how much historicity is enough, but I know God does, and has looked after the matter.) But it does not follow that the investigation of the Old Testament history is part of doing Old Testament theology. The subject matter for Old Testament theology is the canonical writings.[24]

Therefore the story itself must, at least in some way, refer to real or historical events that actually happened. Goldingay argues that this historical foundation to the story is crucial; however, he argues wisely that OT theology proper need not be founded solely on historical reconstruction. Again Bauckham points out the key issue:

> While the telling of a story can be true, it can never be adequate to or exhaustive of the reality it renders. In this case, the fact that versions and interpretations multiply—especially in the case of the story of Jesus—is testimony to the importance of not reducing his reality to the limitation of a single rendering. The existence of the four Gospels, not to mention commentary in the apostolic letters, keeps readers aware that Jesus is neither captured in the text nor existent only as a textual construction but that he had and has his own reality to which the texts witness.[25]

Goldingay and Bauckham note the key issue that has begun to separate individuals working within BT3—namely, the degree to which the story shape of Scripture refers to historical events. On one hand Goldingay insists that any theologically trustworthy story must refer to actual events, while on the other hand, as Bauckham notes, such a story cannot exhaustively relay either the events or especially the individuals themselves. The story of Scripture relates to history, but for some, exhibits a quality that speaks beyond history as well.

This observation rests precariously on an active fault line that has been painfully shaking between N. T. Wright and Richard Hays. First during an exchange at the 2008 Society of Biblical Literature meetings in Boston,[26] then, more formally, in the spring of 2010 during the annual Wheaton Theology Conference,[27] the sharp methodological differences between Wright and Hays erupted. During the Boston SBL meetings Wright leveled a surprising

---

24. Ibid., 7–8.

25. Bauckham, "Reading Scripture," 43.

26. In a session reviewing *Seeking the Identity of Jesus: A Pilgrimage*, edited by Richard Hays and Beverly Roberts Gaventa (Grand Rapids: Eerdmans, 2009), N. T. Wright sharply criticized the book's insufficiently historical approach.

27. The papers presented at the Wheaton Conference are now published in *Jesus, Paul and the People of God: A Theological Dialogue with N. T. Wright* (ed. Nicholas Perrin and Richard B. Hays; Downers Grove, IL: InterVarsity Press, 2011).

critique of Hays's *Seeking the Identity of Jesus: A Pilgrimage*. Hays recounts the critique:

> Our "pilgrimage," he said, was overdetermined by dogmatic concerns and theological traditions, and inattentive to the realities of first-century history. Real pilgrims, Tom observed, would get their feet dirty on the dusty roads of ancient Palestine. But this book of essays was instead "a pilgrimage by helicopter," and its authors and editors were "pilgrims with suspiciously clean feet." The result was therefore, in his words, a "pseudo-theological project of non-historical retrieval of Jesus."[28]

Hays took the opportunity to respond to this criticism in his paper at the Wheaton Conference. Hays drew attention to several examples in Wright's work where he clearly makes historical study the ultimate foundation of his understanding of the Bible's narrative coherence. Though Wright understands his method to be useful in the church, Hays argued that the primary "conversation partners for Tom's interpretation of Jesus are not Irenaeus or the Council of Chalcedon, not even the letter to the Hebrews or 1 Peter. Rather, the key conversation partners are Josephus, the Dead Sea Scrolls, 4 Ezra and so on." He concludes that "at this point, Tom's method is much more in sync with the priorities of the academy and less in keeping with the perceptions of the church."[29]

At the end of his Wheaton Conference paper Hays makes some concluding observations regarding his methodological impasse with Wright:

> The fault line between Tom and me on story and history is broadly emblematic of a pervasive ambivalence in contemporary evangelical Christianity. The desire for historical validation of Christian claims stands in some tension with a deeply felt desire for the postmodern recovery of canon and tradition as the necessary hermeneutical framework for understanding both Scripture and the world. Both Tom and I want both things, but we have different ways of seeking to integrate them. On the one hand, Tom insists that without historical investigation of the factuality of the Gospels, the story is vacuous, not least at the level of concrete action in the world. I insist, on the other hand, that without the canonical form of the story, we could never get the historical investigation right in the first place.[30]

It remains to be seen whether these two longtime allies have actually encountered a methodological parting of the ways or if their narrative

---

28. Hays, "Knowing Jesus: Story, History and the Question of Truth," in *Jesus, Paul and the People of God*, 43.
29. Ibid., 47–48.
30. Ibid., 61.

approaches are more similar than they now appear. Sometimes the differences between brothers are greatest within the family, while the neighborhood cannot understand all the fuss. At least in this sharp exchange between Hays and Wright we can mark up somewhat of a spectrum within BT3. Like Dallas, Chicago, and Philadelphia in BT2, here we discover a Haysian and a Wrighten BT3.

THE SUBJECT MATTER OF BIBLICAL THEOLOGY

Rather than historical description (BT1) or redemptive history (BT2), the subject matter of BT3 is the narrative structure discernable within the text itself. Through the NT's use of the OT (intertextuality), BT3 gains access to a theological reading of the Bible by detecting how the story line of the OT was taken up and understood by Christian readers. Coming to a conclusion regarding what the Bible is all about (subject matter) is only possible through gaining access to the narrative unity between the Old and New Testaments through the interpretive practices of the authors of the NT themselves. Especially seen in Hays, working from the narrative coherence of the Bible demonstrates the theological shape of the Bible's unity. Rather than starting with historical or social reconstruction, the theological shape of Scripture surfaces by focusing on the narrative aspect of the NT's interpretation of "Israel's story."

Though Wright's methodology differs from Hays, he too seeks to discern the overall narrative coherence of the Bible. Using the philosophical construct of a "worldview-story"—that is, the implied worldview of the authors/readers surfaced from a deep reading of both canonical and extracanonical texts— Wright comes to appreciate the theology of the Bible through the subject matter of overarching narrative coherence. Wright, more than Hays, depends on reading the stories "behind" and "in" the text for the purpose of proclaiming the story "in front of" the text. Rather than the historical or social context "behind the text," both Hays and Wright view the subject matter of biblical theology as the interconnected story line running "through" the text.

CONCLUSION

The clear strength of BT3 is its focus on the narrative connections between the Old and New Testaments—the overarching unity of the Bible's story. Resisting the historical-critical assumption that the meaning of the text equals the sum of its cultural and historical parts (BT1), a narrative reading of Scripture incorporates such background context and unites it with a robust literary appreciation of how the whole of the Bible renders the story of God. Here a sensitivity to understanding individual passages of Scripture in the light of the whole attempts to offer both a more complete picture of the Bible's actual subject matter as well as a meaningful message for contemporary readers. Yet, BT3 is distinct from older, precritical reading as it is influenced by the modern development of narrative models of meaning in both history and ethics. This connection to a modern narrative understanding of reality enables BT3 to claim more for Scripture than just its overarching narrative unity. The single story told in the Bible actually renders a "world"; it shapes a new reality within which readers are invited to find themselves.

Chapter 6

BIBLICAL THEOLOGY AS WORLDVIEW-STORY: N. T. WRIGHT

Few will be unfamiliar with the influential New Testament scholar N. T. (Nicholas Thomas) Wright (b. 1948), or as he is known on a popular level, Tom Wright. Until his recent appointment as Research Professor and Chair of New Testament at the University of St. Andrews, Wright was the Anglican Bishop of Durham. He received his DPhil and DD degrees from Oxford and taught NT studies for twenty years at Cambridge, McGill, and Oxford Universities. Before serving his tenure as Bishop of Durham, Wright was Canon Theologian of Westminster Abbey and before that dean of Lichfield Cathedral.

Wright has established himself as one of the most influential Bible scholars today. His popular and influential *For Everyone* commentary series covers most of the NT. He is an international expert on the historical Jesus, now especially on the resurrection, and is one of the more prominent voices within the so-called "New Perspective" on Paul. Furthermore, his projected six-volume series *Christian Origins and the Question of God* (of which three volumes are complete) offers an account of the origins and development of the early Christian movement along with a comprehensive interpretation of the texts of the NT within this period. Wright's holistic reading of the NT has lead Alister McGrath to note:

> In an age in which much New Testament scholarship is fragmentary in nature, focusing on isolated elements of the New Testament or its themes, Wright's comprehensive approach must be welcomed as a salutary antidote

to the tunnel vision that so often seems to characterize modern New Testament scholarship.[1]

Because of Wright's synthetic approach to the NT specifically and to the Bible in general, he serves as an apt example of doing biblical theology. However, framing Wright's overall project in terms of biblical theology is not straightforward because he has not explicitly written on the subject of biblical theology and never refers to his work as biblical theology. Yet, as we will see below, a key characteristic of his approach is to read the NT within the larger picture of Second Temple Judaism and Israel's Scriptures, understanding them as constitutive of an overarching worldview—clearly a type of biblical theology.

DEFINING THE TASK: TWO PILLARS IN WRIGHT'S OVERARCHING PROJECT

Throughout his voluminous publications, Wright self-consciously argues that the literary category of "story" gives balance to history and theology in reading Scripture. He insists: "To be truly Christian, [theology] must show that it includes the story which the Bible tells, and the sub-stories within it. Without this, it lapses into a mere *ad hoc* use of the Bible, finding bits and pieces to fit into a scheme derived from elsewhere."[2] His concern with the "mere *ad hoc* use of the Bible" moves beyond petty hermeneutical fussiness because reading the Bible as disconnected "bits and pieces" results in mishearing the clear voice of Scripture. When the Bible is read in a fragmented way, readers tend to hear a particular church tradition, or worse, their own voices, instead of those of Jesus or Paul. Two pillars support Wright's project here: "story" and "worldview." First we will consider Wright's use of "story" in biblical theology.

What sets Wright's approach apart from the "tunnel vision" of modern NT scholarship is his ability to set a particular passage into the larger framework of early Christian origins. Like a backdrop on a movie set, the "story" or larger worldview is the crucial setting within which the action of the NT unfolds. In order for one to understand what Jesus or Paul is doing in the scene, one must frame the action within the correct context. Using a different image, that of a mosaic, Wright is concerned that much of modern biblical scholarship has

---

1. Alister E. McGrath, "Reality, Symbol and History: Theological Reflections on N. T. Wright's Portrayal of Jesus," in *Jesus and the Restoration of Israel* (Downers Grove, IL: InterVarsity Press, 1999), 159.
2. Wright, *New Testament and the People of God*, 138.

missed the big picture for all the fragments of glass embedded in the mortar. Though Wright never refers to his work as biblical theology, this "big-picture" perspective aligns with the central concerns of biblical theology, especially with regard to the relationship between the OT and NT along with biblical theology's concern to read Christian Scripture as a coherent whole.

So a key element of Wright's overall project is a clear understanding of this backdrop or mosaic — the worldview-story that stands behind Jesus, Paul, and the NT. Wright argues about his project:

> [It] will involve the discernment and analysis, at one level or another, of first-century stories and their implications. Stories, both in shape and in the manner of their telling, are the crucial agents that invest "events" with "meaning." The way the bare physical facts are described, the point at which tension or climax occurs, the selection of an arrangement — all these indicate the meaning which the event is believed to possess. Our overall task is to discuss the historical origin of Christianity, and, in complex relation to that, the theological question of "god" [sic]; and the thicket where the quarry hides, in each case, may be labeled Story. For the historian, trying to understand the worldview, mindset, motivation and intention ... of Jesus, of Paul and of the evangelists, to hunt for the quarry means not least to understand the stories the characters were telling, both verbally in their preaching and writing, and in action in the paths they chose to tread; to see how these stories worked.[3]

Whereas Wright's "story" is comprehensive and cohesive, it is not artificially systematic. Though Christian theology is important for Wright, he resists defining theology as the arrangement of propositions or timeless truths into a too-neat-and-tidy system of thought. For Wright, this is too abstract and, in the end, artificially imposed on the text rather than naturally emanating from it. Instead, for Wright Christian theology must clearly announce the biblical story, the true story about the Creator and his world; it is the story of what this Creator has done and is doing to redeem his people and ultimately to restore his good creation. For him, doctrines of systematic theology are actually "portable stories," something like suitcases that travel well, but they are packed full of implied narrative.[4]

But the biblical "story" that theology tells is a particular story for Wright. With respect to his work on Paul, Wright describes how this "story" should be formulated:

---

3. Ibid., 79.
4. N. T. Wright, "Reading Paul, Thinking Scripture," in *Scripture's Doctrine and Theology's Bible: How the New Testament Shapes Christian Dogmatics* (ed. Markus Bockmuehl and Alan J. Torrance; Grand Rapids: Baker, 2008), 62–64.

What I am arguing for is an approach to Pauline Theology [or the Bible in general] which will neither on the one hand reduce this strange entity to a mere function of social forces or rhetorical conventions, nor on the other hand subsume it under the traditional *loci* of a different age (whether the sixteenth or any other century). The right approach will, rather, grapple with the task of understanding Paul's own thought-forms and thought-patterns, as a Pharisee and then as a Christian, and attempt to restate them coherently in such a way as to show their proper interrelation, with his total world-view, without doing them violence en route.[5]

Here we can decipher how Wright might align the concerns of history and theology under the rubric of "story." He wants to balance genuine historical inquiry into the text while at the same time open up understanding of the text to theological realities.[6] However, these theological realities are built on "Paul's own thought-forms" and "thought-patterns." Discerning Paul's "thought-forms" and "thought-patterns" focuses on a *historical* reconstruction of the worldview of the Judaism Paul found himself living in contrasted with the emerging Christian worldview derived from the life, death, and resurrection of Jesus. Here Wright's version of biblical theology is reading the text against the backdrop of the *historically* reconstructed "story" of Israel's Scriptures.

Working alongside the notion of story is that of "worldview." For Wright, worldviews operate on a presuppositional or precognitive level, "like the foundations of a house: vital, but invisible."[7] These foundational presuppositions, in turn, are expressed through stories ("worldview-by-means-of-story"). He argues that "worldviews provide the *stories* through which human beings view reality. Narrative is the most characteristic expression of worldview, going deeper than the isolated observation or fragmented remark."[8] Thus, he notes, through stories "one can in principle discover how to answer the basic questions that determine human existence: who are we, where are we, what is wrong, and what is the solution."[9] For Wright, then, stories express a worldview and in turn generate theological beliefs. Therefore, in Wright's understanding stories form a foundation supporting basic presuppositions (in the form of a worldview)

---

5. N. T. Wright, *The Climax of the Covenant: Christ and the Law in Pauline Theology* (Minneapolis: Fortress, 1993), 17.

6. Wright attempts to place his project in the academic context: "To put it another way, we need to do justice, simultaneously, to Wrede's emphasis on serious history (including the history of Jesus), Bultmann's emphasis on normative theology, and the postmodern emphasis on the text and its readers. Each of these, of course, is inclined to claim sole rights, and to resent sharing territory it regards as its own. But such grandiose claims should be resisted" (*New Testament and the People of God*, 27).

7. Ibid., 125.

8. Ibid., 123 (emphasis original).

9. Ibid.

that then become fixed in theological convictions.[10] Thus, a "story" and the "worldview" it produces is central to Wright's notion of biblical theology.

Standing just beside the "worldview-story" pillar is Wright's approach to epistemology—a position he labels "critical realism." Though Wright neither pioneered this position nor was the first to apply it to the realm of biblical studies, he surely is responsible for making it popular. Both terms—"critical" and "realism"—note a particular response to the excesses of both modernity and postmodernity. The "critical" part of critical realism rejects the notion that basic "facts" about the world are transparently and objectively known by the neutral historian or scientist (i.e., historical positivism). This position is hopelessly naïve. Here Wright, along with many others, is pushing back against the overconfidence of post-Enlightenment objective science. Rather than absolute objective knowledge, the "critical" in critical realism acknowledges that all human knowing is finite and, in the end, incomplete.

On the other side, critical realism pushes back the tide of radical postmodernity, with its claim that because all knowing is incomplete and partial, certainty is impossible. The "realism" of critical realism firmly claims that there is something there to know, real knowledge that is not merely already a part of the knower's perception. Richard Hays describes critical realism as "an epistemologically chastened position that recognizes both the role of the human agent's worldview in shaping perception ... and, at the same time, the reality of the external world perceived by that agent." Largely appreciative of this aspect of Wright's project, Hays continues: "Through a process of trial and error, the testing of 'fit' between worldview and evidence, the knower can gradually attain a reasonably accurate picture of the real world, including the real world of past history."[11]

This accurate knowledge of the "real world of past history" is precisely the goal for Wright. While acknowledging the difficulty and incompleteness of our knowledge of the Bible, he insists that literary and historical tools are up to the task of accurately reconstructing the worldview-story within which real knowledge about the life of Jesus may be known. Throughout his writings, Wright carefully explores his starting assumptions and methodology. The two pillars of "story" (or as we are labeling it, "worldview-story") and "critical realism" constitute foundational starting points for understanding Wright's overall project.

---

10. Wright develops this further in *Jesus and the Victory of God* (London: SPCK, 1996), 138: "Worldviews are the lenses through which a society looks at the world, the grid upon which are plotted the multiple experiences of life."

11. Hays, "Knowing Jesus," 46.

THE WRIGHT STORY: CONSTRUCTION OF THE "WORLDVIEW-STORY"

Because this notion of worldview-story is so important in Wright's practice of biblical theology, we must explore it further. Wright's worldview-story is first *historically* rooted and emerges particularly from the context of Second Temple Judaism (i.e., Jewish practice and belief from the reconstruction of the temple in c. 520 BC up to the destruction of the same in AD 70). Wright argues:

> The task of the historian is not simply to assemble little clumps of "facts" and hope that somebody else will integrate them. The historian's job is to show their interconnectedness, that is, how one thing follows from another, precisely by examining the "inside" of the events.... To display this, the historian needs (it will come as no surprise) to tell a story.[12]

Crucial to Wright's task is to set the stories of the NT within the context of the grand, worldview-stories the early Christians told and retold. "The early Christians were *story-tellers*. There were plenty of philosophies on offer in the ancient world whose commitment to stories was less obvious than theirs.... With the early Christians ... stories were visibly and obviously an essential part of what they were and did."[13]

Here the Christian stories are the full-length accounts of Jesus' life, the Gospels themselves. These texts, Wright insists, do tell us about Jesus, but to understand them correctly Wright would have us read these larger stories within the overarching, grand worldview-story of Second Temple Judaism. Here Wright's methodology is much more sophisticated than attempting to compile as many parallels between the biblical literature and Second Temple sources. Whereas it is common for NT scholars to rummage about for parallels between Second Temple Judaism and the NT (characteristic of BT1), Wright undertakes this strategy on a grand scale. He does not merely compile individual parallels between, for example, the gospel of Luke and the Dead Sea Scrolls, but he attempts to see the implicit worldview bound up within the documents of Second Temple Judaism and in turn uses this (historically) reconstructed worldview as a hermeneutical tool for understanding the entire Bible. Here Hays defends Wright's use of such parallels, arguing that Wright "is not merely mining ancient Jewish texts for parallels to this or that saying of Jesus. Rather he is consistently reading them with an eye to discerning their worldview, asking about the story they tell about God, Israel and the world."[14]

---

12. Wright, *New Testament and the People of God*, 113–14; see pp. 113–18, which unpacks this in detail.
13. Ibid., 372 (emphasis original).
14. Hays, "Knowing Jesus," 47–48.

In order to reconstruct the worldview-story that acts as the backdrop for Jesus and Paul, one must painstakingly stitch the smaller stories together. But crucial in understanding Wright, one must inquire from where these smaller stories might come. Rather than finding one common theme woven through the Old and New Testaments and then using this theme as the backdrop for Jesus and Paul (as in BT2), Wright's worldview-story is historically rooted in both canonical and extracanonical texts. That is to say, Wright's worldview-story is not merely constructed by piecing together the voices of the biblical authors themselves, but placing those biblical stories against the backdrop of the larger story of God and his people primarily told by Second Temple Judaism.

For example, Wright contends that Israel's worldview-story was "inevitably read in the Second-Temple period as a story in search of a conclusion. This ending would have to incorporate the full liberation and redemption of Israel, an event which had not happened as long as Israel was being oppressed, a prisoner in her own land."[15] He supports this hypothesis by showing both the reflection of continuing exile found in the postexilic documents in the OT and by citing the "proposed endings" offered in the noncanonical sources of Josephus, Sirach, and the Maccabees.[16] Drawing these sources together into one comprehensive narrative, Wright argues that the symbols in this worldview-story stood as cultural landmarks reminding Israel of where she had come from, where she was, and where she was to be going. Israel's notion of who they were was wrapped up in the symbols of temple, land, Torah, and election. Though the temple had been rebuilt and a great number had returned to the land, Wright detects in these Second Temple stories the abiding expectation of the full restoration of God's people.

For example, he points out that nothing similar to the coming of God's Shekinah, his glorious presence in 1 Kings 8:10–11, had been experienced in the new temple, and therefore Israel viewed the exile as still in progress. Ezekiel's vision is one in which the Lord inhabits the temple in the future:

> The Spirit lifted me up and brought me into the inner court; and behold, the glory of the LORD filled the temple. While the man was standing beside me, I heard one speaking to me out of the temple, and he said to me, "Son of man, this is the place of my throne and the place of the soles of my feet, where I will dwell in the midst of the people of Israel forever." (Ezek 43:5–7a)

This promised vision of Ezekiel was not understood to have been fulfilled within Second Temple Judaism and therefore should be seen as future hope.

---

15. Wright, *New Testament and the People of God*, 217.
16. Ibid., 217–18.

In short, though Israel had returned to the land and had rebuilt the temple, they continued to see themselves as exiles: "Behold, we are slaves this day; in the land that you gave to our fathers to enjoy its fruit and its good gifts, behold, we are slaves (Neh 9:36)."

Wright then reads Jesus' life and ministry against the backdrop of Israel's story of expected restoration from its continuing exile. Specifically attempting to understand Jesus' invitation to repent against Wright's reconstructed worldview-story, he challenges the Christian view of repentance derived from systematic theology. He claims repentance understood as a purely individual, moral turning from evil and rebellious conduct is wrongheaded and involves a caricature of Judaism. Rather, repentance should be viewed within the worldview-story of Second Temple Judaism constructed from canonical and noncanonical sources. Specifically repentance should be seen as *"what Israel must do if her exile [was] to come to an end."*[17]

Supporting this notion of repentance, Wright asserts the Greek word "repentance" and its cognates are rare in the Septuagint and that when they do occur, the context speaks of God himself repenting. Furthermore, the word is used of Israel's returning to Yahweh with all her heart in texts such as Deuteronomy 6:4 (along with other references in the Torah [Lev. 26:40–45; Deut. 30:2, 8], the Prophets,[18] postbiblical Judaism, the Qumran documents), which Wright sees as a condition of Israel's forgiveness and return from exile. From this evidence he draws the conclusion that in Jesus' context repentance would have carried the same connotations of what Israel must do in order to be restored from her exile.

From this position Wright attempts to extend his reconstruction of repentance in Jesus' context into what he thinks are practical and specifically political terms. He understands the sin Israel must turn from is her revolutionary zeal. Israel's attempt to obtain restoration on her own terms is the evil that keeps her from experiencing it—an insight, Wright notes, that has been universally overlooked.

In support of this connection, Wright offers as evidence an incident where an attempt was made against Josephus' life by "Jesus the brigand" near Galilee around AD 66. Upon the capture of the brigand, Josephus expresses a willingness to show mercy if "Jesus the brigand" would only "show repentance and prove his loyalty."[19] Wright argues that this example shows repen-

---

17. Wright, *Jesus and the Victory of God*, 248 (emphasis original).
18. Ibid., 248 n.15.
19. Josephus, *Life*, 110 (trans. Thackeray), as quoted by Wright, *Jesus and the Victory of God*, 250.

tance as turning from revolutionary tendencies and confessing "loyalty to" or "belief in" a leader. Therefore, if this was the meaning of repentance in AD 66, it stands to reason the same was true of repentance thirty or forty years earlier. He concludes: "The most plausible historical reconstruction of Jesus' call to repent brings together ... the two emphases we have now sketched (returning to YHWH so that the exile may come to an end; renunciation of nationalist violence)."[20] Thus the renunciation of political violence demonstrated in Josephus serves as a crucial small story, which informs the meaning of repentance in the larger, worldview-story of Second Temple Judaism. The point of this discussion is to provide an example of how Wright uses this reconstructed worldview-story as a hermeneutical lens to formulate his version of biblical theology.

As this example demonstrates, both canonical and noncanonical sources play *equal* roles in constructing the worldview-story through which Wright connects the entire narrative of Scripture. Reflecting on this aspect of Wright's project, Richard Hays notes that integral to Wright's method

> is his broad engagement with Jewish sources from the Second Temple era. These texts and sources allow him to draw the map on which the Jesus of the Gospels is to be located. That map is not the framework of the Christian creedal tradition, or even of the canonical New Testament. Rather it is the "cultural encyclopedia"—the cultural framework of reference—of Jewish religion and culture in the ancient Mediterranean world.[21]

We will return to Hays's assessment of Wright's project below, but here it is key to understand how Wright's "worldview-story" is constructed by means of both canonical and noncanonical sources.

THE WRIGHT CONNECTION BETWEEN THE TESTAMENTS

As the previous section suggests, Wright helpfully connects the Old and New Testaments within his reconstructed worldview-story, notwithstanding his use of canonical and noncanonical texts seemingly with equal authority.[22] Stressing the grand narrative or story of the Old and New Testaments

---

20. Ibid., 251.
21. Hays, "Knowing Jesus," 47–48.
22. For the purposes of historical reconstruction of his "worldview-story," Wright treats both canonical and noncanonical texts equally, though of course when he turns to read the OT and NT through the lens of his "worldview-story" the canonical texts are uniquely authoritative.

obviously draws the two halves of the Bible together, indicating a greater level of continuity. Noting the logic of narrative, Wright argues:

> Not all the biblical books are in narrative form, but the majority are, and the present framing of the canon of scripture ... all emphasize an overarching narrative from a beginning to an end, with various subplots in between, which transcends, though includes, the messages of the individual books.[23]

As such the Old and New Testaments are to be read as one story. Wright argues for this continuity in that the NT consistently presents the story of Jesus as the fulfillment of or climax to the OT narrative. Here OT and NT are connected in an organic—narrative—fashion. Yet it is not obvious how this overarching narrative, Wright's worldview-story, finds its internal cohesion. Though described as an overarching narrative whole, the relationship of the OT to the NT can be described in several different ways. Are the Old and New Testaments connected via allegory, typology, or supersessionism? Though Wright never uses the term, perhaps the most appropriate word to describe his attempt at connecting the OT and the NT would be "continuation."[24]

> In the Christian canonical Bible as we now have it we find, without much difficulty, a single over-arching narrative. It is the story which runs from creation to new creation, from Eden to the New Jerusalem.[25]

For Wright, both NT and OT tell the same story, not two stories. He sees the OT as a "story in search of an ending. It ends with a sort of 'Yes, and what next?'" Left with such narratival incompleteness Wright outlines this "continuation," specifically how the "what next" question is explicitly answered in the NT:

> The Christian canon as we have it is that same story, with the four gospels saying, in their very different ways, this is the climax of the story, and then the Epistles and the Apocalypse, saying "Now this is what we do with it." With the end of Revelation providing this wonderful image of the heavenly city coming down from heaven to earth, we don't end by going back to Eden, instead there is the climax of the story, with the human project, God's project, finished successfully. That's the big story.[26]

---

23. N. T. Wright, "The Bible for the Post-Modern World" (this paper was given as the Latimer Fellowship, Orange Memorial Lecture, 1999) (www.biblicaltheology.ca/blue_files/The%20Bible%20for%20the%20Post%20Modern%20World.pdf; accessed August 2, 2011).

24. Kyle T. Fever's word, "N.T. Wright for Everyone: Biblical Theology," 4 (www.scribd.com/doc/27022370/NT-Wright-on-Biblical-Theology; accessed August 2, 2011).

25. Wright, "The Bible for the Post-Modern World."

26. Ibid.

So the NT continues the story that originated in the OT. As a plot moves forward in time with the succession of event after event, the thread connecting the Old and New Testaments is this narrative progression. It is interesting to note that this progression moves in one direction through time, namely, from Old to New. Furthermore, this historically developing narrative direction is constructed from texts outside the Christian canon and, in Wright's account, focus almost exclusively along the trajectory of exile and return.

THE SCOPE OF BIBLICAL THEOLOGY IN WRIGHT'S WORK

Clearly as one who has served the church for a significant portion of his life, Wright understands the task of biblical theology or of reconstructing the worldview-story of the Bible as directly impinging on modern life. Setting the groundwork for *The New Testament and the People of God*, Wright notes, "The aim … is to suggest what might be involved in a 'theological' reading that does not bypass the 'literary' and 'historical' readings, but rather enhances them; and to explore one possible model of letting this composite reading function as normative or authoritative."[27] He expands on what this normative aspect of biblical theology might look like in his efforts:

> What then might a specifically *Christian* theology be? More, I take it, than simply an account of what Christians have believed in the past, or believe in the present, though those tasks will always be part of the whole. That whole includes a necessarily normative element. It will attempt not just to describe but to commend a way of looking at, speaking about, and engaging with the god in whom Christians believe, and with the world that this god has created. It will carry the implication that this *is* not only what is believed but what *ought to be* believed.[28]

Though Wright clearly stresses that biblical theology is a normative task, his version of biblical theology is almost exclusively narrative, or consists of his reconstructed worldview-story. Thus, one might ask, How is a "story" authoritative or normative?

Wright offers what has become a famous metaphor in describing how the worldview-story of Scripture functions as a normative and authoritative "story." He suggests the hypothetical situation where a Shakespearean play is discovered, but most of the final, fifth act is missing. The decision to stage the play is made. The first four acts and the remnant of the fifth act are given

---

27. Wright, *New Testament and the People of God*, 121.
28. Ibid., 131 (emphasis original).

to skillful and experienced Shakespearean actors, who immerse themselves both in the first part of the play and in the culture and time of Shakespeare. They are asked to work out the concluding fifth act in keeping both with the first four acts and with what they already know of Shakespeare. This conclusion must be both consistent, in tune with the first four acts, and, at the same time, innovative. It cannot merely be a rehearsing of the previous acts, no mere repetition. As faithful improvisation, the actors must act out an authentic conclusion in the fifth and final act.[29]

For Wright this becomes a way of telling both a public and comprehensive story, which in turn is authoritative. Understanding Scripture as a connected narrative (like a five-act play) connects to a particular worldview—the story paints the world as it is in reality. It is public in that it conveys information about the world itself, not just about a particular individual—it claims to tell *the* story of how the world really is.[30] It is also comprehensive: it is able to take account of the various aspects of life and makes sense—it describes a compelling logic—of them as a cohesive whole. This comprehensive and public worldview-story, then, is authorized. That is, it is given authority to tell the story of the real, public world like it is. As with the analogy of the Shakespearean play, the narrative of Scripture acts as a controlling story for all of life—it is in this way that Scripture is normative. This worldview-story of Scripture is normative for the Christian community today.

It is here that one can see Wright's particular take on biblical theology. He would have the biblical story become the controlling story for biblical scholarship. Yet, as we have seen the particular worldview-story, Wright works with what is reconstructed on the back of a very historical understanding of time (diachronic development; e.g., reading the OT first, then the NT) and texts outside the Christian canon. Whether this is the most proper way to construct a "story" from which to broker space between history and theology, the observation at least may beg the question of who is actually qualified to do this kind of worldview-story reading of Scripture.

DOING THE TASK: WHO IS QUALIFIED TO DO BIBLICAL THEOLOGY?

One might assume, judging by his own example, that Wright would argue such a reading of Scripture would be done both in the church and in the

---

29. See ibid., 142–43.
30. This narrative told in Scripture "offers a story which is the story of the whole world. It is public truth" (ibid., 41–42).

academy. He claims, "narrative theology, or telling the story will be a neces-sary part of the church's task as they live in 'act five' of the biblical story."[31] In general, a biblical theology as worldview-story can play a role in making the church—including biblical scholars—aware of the overarching story in the Bible and which in turn ought to shape Christian life. However, Wright's approach is not merely a narrative biblical theology. His worldview-story is manufactured with material (Second Temple Jewish sources) and blueprints (hermeneutical assumptions about worldview and "story") with which the average church leader is not trained to work. Here the assessment of Richard Hays we quoted earlier rings in the ear:

> The important conversation partners for Tom's interpretation of Jesus are not Irenaeus or the Council of Chalcedon, not even the letter to the Hebrews or 1 Peter. Rather, the key conversation partners are Josephus, the Dead Sea Scrolls, 4 Ezra and so on ... at this point, Tom's method is much more in sync with the priorities of the academy and less in keeping with the percep-tions of the church.[32]

Though Wright would desire that his method be replicated in the church, there is a big question as to whether this is a reasonable expectation. In the end, a fully narrative approach would require both those in the academy and church leadership to work together, the latter using the resources of the for-mer to communicate the conclusions of a proper narrative biblical theology.

ASSESSMENT

Wright's reading of the Old and New Testaments clearly registers on the spectrum of biblical theology as conceived here. His conception of how the "story" of Scripture constitutes the narrative unfolding of God's work in the world is remarkable. As McGrath noted above, Wright stands as an excep-tion within NT studies for the way in which he is able to see how the parts form a coherent whole without doing violence to the parts in order that they fit together. In fact, Wright's contribution is particularly helpful because of his insistence on bringing history and theology together via narrative.[33] On our continuum, Wright's version of BT3 attempts to level out at the perfect middle point between history and theology—the question is whether he actually achieves this difficult balance.

---

31. Ibid., 142.
32. Hays, "Knowing Jesus," 47–48.
33. See especially Wright, *New Testament and the People of God*, 4–5.

Wright's version of biblical theology, though richly narrative in final shape, is ultimately established on the bedrock of history. The worldview-story, which functions for Wright as a key hermeneutical lens, is actually constructed of essentially historical material, which for some constitutes an implicit imbalance away from theological concerns. As Hays's comments above indicate, Wright seems to set the historical study of Scripture as the ultimate foundation of theological understanding. Along with Hays, C. Stephen Evans notes how Wright works with an implicit "methodological naturalism"[34]—that is, Evans thinks Wright's use of history in interpretation is set within the methodological restrictions of naturalistic assumptions about history. Positively, within the scholarly discussion of the biblical texts, such "methodological naturalism" serves Wright well as he wishes to articulate both the unity and the theological subject matter of the Bible in the context of secular history. Negatively, however, Evans notes the cost involved: "there are times when Wright appears to go beyond using this historical method to suggest a much stronger claim: that such a method is the best or even the only means of ascertaining the historical truth about Jesus of Nazareth."[35] Wright's type of BT3 clearly leans heavily toward the history end of the spectrum. Murray Rae highlights the central issue for many who find fault with Wright: "The important question to be considered is whether the faith or dogma informing the New Testament witness obscures or helps to reveal the reality with which we are concerned."[36]

Whereas Richard Hays certainly thinks such dogma helps, Wright clearly is suspicious of such starting points trampling over historically disciplined reading of Scripture. If not in fact, at least in rhetoric Wright advocates for the historical study of the Scriptures as the only way forward in the face of a variety of the church's traditional theological positions. Whereas many of his insights are helpful, his implicit insistence on his own historical method, often at the expense of a traditional theological position, will be a price too high to pay for many.

---

34. C. Stephen Evans, "Methodological Naturalism in Historical Biblical Scholarship," in *Jesus and the Restoration of Israel: A Critical Assessment of N. T. Wright's* Jesus and the Victory of God (ed. Carey C. Newman; Downers Grove, IL: InterVarsity Press, 1999), 180–205.

35. Ibid., 201. Evans's entire discussion is worth reading. See also Wright's rather sharp comments regarding his use of history over against church tradition, "Whence and Whither Historical Jesus Studies in the Life of the Church?" in *Jesus, Paul and the People of God: A Theological Dialogue with N. T. Wright* (ed. Nicholas Perrin and Richard B. Hays; Downers Grove, IL: InterVarsity Press, 2011), 115–58 (esp. 130–33, 137, 141, 143).

36. Murray A. Rae, *History and Hermeneutics* (London: T&T Clark, 2005), 47.

Part 4

TYPE 4: BIBLICAL THEOLOGY AS CANONICAL APPROACH

Chapter 7

BIBLICAL THEOLOGY AS CANONICAL APPROACH: DEFINITION

The fourth type of biblical theology (BT4) works hard to unite the historical and theological dimensions of biblical theology with the foundational axis being the canon. The canonical approach in general strives to articulate a perspective on the relationship between biblical studies and theology. In contrast to BT1, for example, BT4 does not relegate the biblical text as secondary to biblical history. A canonical approach to biblical theology "challenges the assumption that the earliest historical events play such a determinative role in the capacity of scripture to have authority or to render reality."[1] The canon serves to enjoin the historical meaning of the ancient text with the contemporary meaning of Christian Scripture.[2]

The central tenet for the canonical approach is in regards to the Christian "canon." Although the term is often used in other religious traditions, it first arose within Christianity as both a norm and an attribute of Scripture.[3] The term "canon" vacillates between two distinct poles: "between canon as a norm and canon as a list or standardization of text."[4] While canon as a

---

1. Gerald T. Sheppard, "Canonical Criticism," *ABD*, 1:861–66.
2. The canonical approach it not merely concerned with the "Bible," a vague title given to an ancient, historical text, but "Scripture," a title that bequeaths its necessary nature as the contemporary and living Word of God.
3. Gerald T. Sheppard, "Canon," *Encyclopedia of Religion* (ed. Lindsay Jones; Detroit: Macmillan Reference, 2005), 3:1406.
4. Ibid., 3:1410.

standardization of text refers to the external form of Christian Scripture, canon as a norm refers to how Christian Scripture functions in light of its collective form.

The former meaning is what most often comes to mind in regard to the term "canon," but the canonical approach is dealing almost exclusively with the latter. Although "canon" is not identical to "Scripture," the terms are often used interchangeably.[5] While some have argued against such an interchange because of what appears to be the open or unfixed nature of the Jewish Bible (OT), supporters of the canonical approach argue that a distinction between theological and literary determinations in regard to canon "is to misunderstand the role of the church or synagogue in respect of how it handles its sacred inheritance."[6] A canonical interpretation of Scripture, therefore, inevitably *assumes some operational convictions regarding the identity, character, and literary sources of revelation or truth* to which the Christian faith lays claim in the world. This becomes the foundation of the canonical approach.

The canonical approach, or what some have called "canonical criticism," is more like a collection of canonical approaches or criticisms. "There is no more a single, uniform, canonical approach than there is a single, uniform, 'historical-critical method.'"[7] Yet the canonical approach to biblical theology, it has been argued, provides the most realistic and unifying factor of the Bible. This is in contrast to a theme or concept (e.g., the approach of BT2), such as covenant or promise-and-fulfillment, which have all ended in failed attempts to attach a handle to Scripture in order to tame it or manipulate it.[8]

James Sanders first coined and popularized the term "canon criticism."[9] He sought to find a "canonical hermeneutic" that would explain why the same normative traditions could be properly interpreted with contradictory implications at different times and in different places. While Sanders placed what he later called "canonical criticism" alongside the other biblical criticisms, Brevard Childs entirely avoided such a designation and affiliation.

---

5. For example, according to Albert C. Sundberg Jr., *The Old Testament of the Early Church* (HTS 20; Cambridge, MA: Harvard Univ. Press, 1964), 130: "The uncertainty in the church about the extent of the Old Testament could not have arisen if the extent of the Old Testament had already been fixed in the time of Jesus and of the primitive church."

6. Christopher R. Seitz, *The Character of Christian Scripture: The Significance of a Two-Testament Bible* (STI; Grand Rapids: Baker, 2011), 74. Cf. Brevard S. Childs, *Biblical Theology of the Old and New Testaments* (Minneapolis: Fortress, 1993), 55–69.

7. Anthony C. Thiselton, "Canon, Community, and Theological Construction: Introduction," in *Canon and Biblical Interpretation* (ed. Craig G. Barthomomew et al.; SHS 7; Grand Rapids: Zondervan/Milton Keyes, UK: Paternoster, 2006), 1–30 (4).

8. James A. Sanders, *From Sacred Story to Sacred Text: Canon as Paradigm* (Philadelphia: Fortress, 1987), 4.

9. James A. Sanders, *Torah and Canon* (Philadelphia: Fortress, 1972).

Childs preferred to speak of a "canonical approach," which for him high-lighted how "the canonical shape" of a biblical book established possibilities and limits to its interpretation as Scripture.[10] Others have suggested at least a "canon conscious" exegesis, which seeks to elaborate on the inner-biblical interpretive issues at play in the canon of Scripture.[11]

Amidst the diversity of canonical approaches, what is uniform is a her-meneutical, historical, and theological approach to canon in order to deter-mine its diverse uses and applications. Rather than merely grasping for the prehistory (compositional history) of the biblical text, "scholars start with the canonical context as a way to assess how earlier traditions have been put together to form a new literary entity."[12] The canon is a path that has been traversed by many travelers, each of whom has left many footprints. The final form of the canon, therefore, is a collection of tradition "handlings," with the final form being the last shaping of the tradition. In this way the canon preserves a collection of "tradition shapings," which maintain fidelity to the original material and simultaneously promote the adaptation of the material for a new setting and situation.

> A canonical context of the Bible exhibits moments of both formal preserva-tion and contextual modification, both historical retention and ahistorical, or topical reorientation.... This transformation in the meaning of texts and traditions occurs through a complex, sociopolitical process of literary produc-tion leading to the public recognition of both a particular religion and the canonization of its scripture. This process ... reflects in general terms a dialec-tical relationship between canon and community, between the formation of a scripture and the identification of the community of faith that treasures it.[13]

For this reason the dynamic canon itself becomes the overarching context used to determine the meaning of Scripture. The locus of meaning no longer resides entirely, even primarily, with the original, historical context, but in the canon, which contains the remnants of the original context, but also the

---

10. For a helpful comparison between Brevard Childs and James Sanders, see Frank W. Spina, "Canonical Criticism: Childs Versus Sanders" in *Interpreting God's Word for Today: An Inquiry into Hermeneutics from a Biblical Theological Perspective* (ed. Wayne McCown and James Earl Massey; Anderson, IN: Warner, 1982), 165–94.

11. Cf. I. L. Seeligmann, "Voraussetzung der Midraschexegese," *SVTQ* 1 (1953): 150–81.

12. Sheppard, "Canonical Criticism," 1:863.

13. Ibid., 1:862. The dialectical relationship between canon and community does not give the contem-porary community of faith, for example, the patent to do what it wills with the witness of the Bible. Rather, alongside the longstanding community of faith, the interpretation of the canon is seen to be guided by the Rule of Faith, which was (and continues to be) determined by the church to be the hypothesis, order, and arrangement of Scripture. This rule guards against anything that would chal-lenge "the maximal authority of the Scriptures" (Seitz, The *Character of Christian Scripture*, 196).

revised remains of other historical contexts to which it was applied throughout its scriptural history. Said another way, the meaning of Scripture is not located behind the text but in the canonical form of the text itself.

Even more, this canonical form contains not only some of the original written record but also some of the revisions, which reflect how the past meaning was received and has been understood (developmentally) into the present. Thus, BT4 is concerned that other types of biblical theology have neglected important questions regarding the form and function of the Bible as a living Scripture. BT4 makes certain that the canon is the primary, mediating category for biblical theology. We are entitling BT4 as "Biblical Theology as Canonical Approach," since its method is entirely focused on the interpretive control and function of the biblical canon.

THE TASK OF BIBLICAL THEOLOGY

It is commonly assumed that the responsible interpreter must start with the historical or descriptive task and then establish a bridge to the theological or prescriptive task. Such a starting point usually places the hermeneutical challenges at the feet of the theological, prescriptive task, since the historical, descriptive task is assumed to be self-evident. As argued by proponents of BT4, however, the reverse is more often the case. "The basic issue revolves around the definition of the descriptive task."[14] What is the content that is being described and what tools are needed to perform this task? BT4 begins, therefore, by (re)defining the nature of the descriptive and prescriptive tasks of exegesis and biblical theology, seeking to be appropriate to both sides of the interpretive coin. For BT4, the only bridge between both tasks is the biblical canon. Stated succinctly, *the task of BT4 is to affirm the exegetical form and function of the canon for biblical theology, embracing both the descriptive (historical) and prescriptive (theological) nature of Scripture and its confessional community.* This can be supported by several necessary explanations.

First, biblical theology is not primarily concerned with the brute facts of biblical history but with the faithful, theological construal of these events in canonical form. Unlike BT1, which sought to interpret the Bible against—and only against—the reconstructed historical past, BT4 understands the context of the Bible to be not only multifaceted, but also primarily detectable within the canon, not outside of it. The key to this understanding is what is meant

---

14. See Brevard S. Childs, "Interpretation in Faith: The Theological Responsibility of an Old Testament Commentary," *Int* 18 (1964): 432–49 (437).

by "canon." For the canonical approach, the canon is not defined narrowly as a historical problem that focused on the establishment of the boundaries of a religious tradition's sacred writings, but more broadly as "the complex process involved in the religious usage of tradition," which extends simultaneously back to its canonical beginning and forward to its contemporary canonical function.[15]

For this reason BT4's interest in the "biblical author" is not identical to the "historical author" reconstructed by modern historical criticism. Rather, the biblical author is to be seen behind the carefully woven reapplication of the tradition in different settings, which no single author, not even the original author, can encompass. The focus is intentionally and purposefully on the text itself. The text is not a window for viewing another object; the text *is* the object. Ultimately the canonical approach

> seeks neither to use the text merely as a source for other information ... nor to reconstruct a history of religions development. Rather, it treats the literature in its own integrity ... to do justice to a literature ... not [to] make any dogmatic claims for the literature apart from the literature itself.[16]

Second, biblical theology implies a close, almost interweaving relationship between the Old and New Testaments as part of a single canon of Scripture. For the Christian, the first Testament is no longer the Hebrew Scripture but the Christian OT. This fact signals not merely a functional relationship with the NT, but an essential one. As Childs explains:

> The New Testament in relating the message of the Gospel to the Jewish Scripture goes far beyond asserting its relationship in terms of a historical sequence ... moving the discourse to an ontological plane.... The term ontological refers to a mode of speech in relation to a subject matter which disregards or transcends temporal sequence.[17]

By diluting the historical, linear connection of the Testaments, the interpreter must see both Testaments as essential parts of the Christian Bible. The OT, as much as the NT, must remain authoritative for the church. While the canonical form of the Bible warrants a respect for the two *distinct voices* of the Testaments, the Christian church simultaneously affirms that the Bible is a

---

15. Brevard S. Childs, "Response to Reviewers of *Introduction to the Old Testament as Scripture*," *JSOT* 16 (1980), 52–60 (53).

16. Brevard S. Childs, *Introduction to the Old Testament as Scripture* (Philadelphia: Fortress, 1979), 73.

17. Brevard S. Childs, "Does the Old Testament Witness to Jesus Christ?" in *Evangelium, Schriftauslegung, Kirche: Festschrift für Peter Stuhlmacher zum 65. Geburtstag* (ed. Jostein Ådna, Scott J. Hafemann, and Otfried Hofius (Göttingen: Vandenhoeck & Ruprecht, 1997), 57–64 (59–60).

unified witness bearing testimony to one Lord, Jesus Christ, who is, at the core of both Testaments, the divine reality underlying the entire biblical canon.[18]

Third, biblical theology assumes a particular perspective on "Scripture" and its relation to the history of religious interpretation and theology. The canonical approach seeks to determine how the Bible, as an ancient text, is still normative for today. A central tenet for the canonical approach is that the canon serves as Scripture not merely for the original audience, but also for the contemporary audience; the same Scripture is Scripture for all ages. As Sanders explains:

> The model canonical criticism sponsors as more nearly true to what happened, and what happens, is that of the Holy Spirit as working all along the path of the canonical process: from original speaker, through what was understood by hearers; to what disciples believed was said; to how later editors reshaped the record, oral or written, of what was said; on down to modern hearings and understandings of the texts in current believing communities.[19]

The context of the Bible today is not merely the ancient, historical context but also the Bible in contemporary believing communities. Thus, as Sanders suggests, "canonical criticism may permit the current believing communities to see themselves more clearly as heirs of a very long line of shapers and reshapers of tradition and instruct the faithful as to how they may faithfully perceive the Bible even yet as adaptable for life."[20] The normative canon serves to contextualize the Bible in the contemporary church without demoting or denying the previous contextualizations and applications since the beginning of the Christian movement.

Canon, therefore, is not merely a listing of received books, but it involves the process by which Christian texts (the Scriptures) were received, collected, transmitted, and shaped. Such a description is not intending to deny that

---

18. Brevard S. Childs, "Toward Recovering Theological Exegesis," *Ex Auditu* 16 (2000): 121–29 (125). For a full and contemporary presentation see Seitz, *The Character of Christian Scripture.*

19. James A. Sanders, *Canon and Community: A Guide to Canonical Criticism* (Philadelphia: Fortress Press, 1984), xvii.

20. Ibid., 20. See also Sanders, *From Sacred Story to Sacred Text*, 63: "The believing communities engage in dialogue with the Bible as canon, out of their own ever-changing contexts, asking two questions: Who are we and what are we to do? The fact that the biblical canon functions in this way issues in three basic observations. (1) In a lengthy process of canonization the Bible emerged out of the experiences of ancient Israel, early Judaism, and the early church, when they asked those two questions of their own authoritative traditions. (2) It was shaped in and by those communities in their common life, cultic and cultural. (3) Its proper function continues to be that of being in dialogue with the heirs of those same communities as they continue to seek answers to those two questions (identity and lifestyle, faith and obedience)."

various versions of the canonical approach define quite differently the nature of contextualization and application, and the nature of the formal relationship between canon and the contemporary community of faith (e.g., Sanders vs. Childs). Rather, it is an attempt to make clear an agreeable emphasis: between canon and confessing church runs a life-supporting umbilical cord through which the necessary nutrients flow both ways. "Canon owes its life to its dialogue with those believing communities; and the believing communities owe their life to their dialogue with it."[21]

THE USE OF BIBLICAL THEOLOGY

The task of biblical theology for BT4 is to focus on the canon, which means that it is not only connected to the academic community, but also necessarily to the confessing Christian church. The academy is needed to explore the textual traditions that have been received, collected, transmitted, and shaped throughout different times, cultures, and languages; the confessing church is needed as the applied audience for whom the texts serve as their life for identity and obedience.

Unfortunately for BT4, the academy and the church have for centuries been bitter opponents. They are like Jacob and Esau, with older brother church losing his inheritance to younger brother university. For this reason there has been much confusion regarding the canonical approach. On the one hand, the canon is a historical configuration that could be claimed by the academy. On the other hand, the canon is a theological configuration that could be claimed by the confessing church. The academy's canon demands for it to be naturalized "so that it comes to be regarded as an arbitrary or accidental feature of the Christian religion, to be explained, not transcendentally, but simply in terms of the immanent process of religious history."[22] The academy's canon, ultimately, will be read diachronically, taking into account the entire past of the text, both original and redacted.

By contrast, the church's canon demands something far more transcendent. The church's canon needs to be read as Scripture; that is, it needs to be read in the particular ways and with the particular virtues that are appropriate to the nature of the inspired and authoritative text, which serves to instruct and edify the saints. Canon is authoritative for the church because it is the instrument of divine address. This instrument also, therefore, makes "a claim that the assembled texts constitute a whole, and that their collection

---

21. Sanders, *From Sacred Story to Sacred Text*, 172.
22. John Webster, "Canon," in *DTIB*, 97–100 (98).

is of significance for the interpretation of the constituent parts."[23] Thus, the academy's historical and immanent approach to the canonical documents conflicts with the church's theological-confessional and transcendent approach to the canonical Scriptures, leaving the canonical approach between the "Rock" (the apostle Peter) and a "hard place" (the university).

The key component for resolution, or at least for an understanding, is the starting place. Simply to begin in the academy, in the canon's historical domain, gives neither the neutrality that is so often assumed nor the semblance of objectivity. As Childs warns:

> One starts on neutral ground, without being committed to a theological position, and deals with textual, historical, and philological problems of the biblical sources before raising the theological issue. But, in point of fact, by defining the Bible as a "source" for objective research the nature of the content to be described has been already determined. *A priori*, it has become a part of a larger category of phenomena. The possibility of genuine theological exegesis has been destroyed from the outset.[24]

For Childs, only when one begins with "an explicit framework of faith"[25] can one truly perform the exegetical task, one that involves both historical and theological dimensions. A truly combined effort must disallow one side getting the (categorical) advantage; both dimensions must be in play from the beginning. Thus, the academy and the church must learn to be partners, not enemies.

What, then, does this partnership look like for the canonical approach? Christopher Seitz defines it in three overlapping areas: literary/exegetical, catholic/ecclesial, and theological.[26] The first area is literary/exegetical. Since the canonical approach is derived from the historical-critical interpretation of the last two centuries, "it shares a concern for the objective reality of the text and for its intentional direction and ruled character."[27] This objective reality, however, is not to be sought behind the text, at the level of the text's reconstructed prehistory, even though it must be dealt with constructively and with theological sensitivity. For example, "a canonical reading can seek to understand the theology of the final-form presentation as a kind of commentary on the text's prehistory."[28] Said more simply, like an expert mechanic can see both the original parts that remain of an engine and also

---

23. Ibid., 99–100.
24. Childs, "Interpretation in Faith," 437.
25. Ibid., 438.
26. Christopher Seitz, "Canonical Approach," in *DTIB*, 100–102.
27. Ibid., 100.
28. Ibid.

the used/rebuilt parts added much later, so also is the canonical approach sensitive to a text's original parts and later additions in order to understand the history and current condition of the "textual engine."

In this way the canonical approach balances the final form of the text with the arrangement and sequencing it exhibits, seeing the final form itself as a statement, all the while competent to judge and constrain the prehistory reconstructed by atheological, historical-critical methods.[29] This literary/exegetical area of the canonical approach looks very much like traditional historical criticism, except that it constrains historical criticism with theological presuppositions and controls.

The second area is catholic/ecclesial. While a canonical approach accepts and utilizes the historical-critical method, it does not think the method by itself satisfactory. Simply stated, historical criticism "only asks specific kinds of questions of texts, it has a different understanding of what counts for good reading."[30] For this reason the canonical approach is open to learn from the past. Rather than moving past or beyond that which came before, the canonical approach is interested in the kinds of questions that occupied theological readers in the rich heritage of the church. Ultimately, as necessary as a historical reading is, it cannot be the rule. A catholic/ecclesial reading is a Christian reading, rooted in an appeal to the "Rule of Faith." This rule—a "measuring rod" used to interpret the Bible rooted in the overarching story of the Bible and its primary subject matter: the gospel of Jesus Christ—functioned in the early church as a hermeneutical key for the interpretation of Scripture. For this reason the canonical approach can never read the Bible in an academic setting alone, for it ultimately requires the confessing church.

The third area is theological. Since the canonical approach is necessarily ecclesial, that about which it speaks is necessarily divine. Theology does not merely confine historical-critical methods or include ancient Christians; it is the topic being addressed. Such a reading forces the context of the Bible to include its entire witness. That is, its full reference must include not only events of history, but also the transcendent God and his assembled people. For this reason the church embraced and claimed as their own the Jewish Scriptures, for from their perspective it was out of the fullness of the revelation that they were able to see the parts fitting within the whole. A true theology of the Bible, contra BT1, for example, is not a theology for the original readers in their historical context alone, but a theology for the entire church with a multifaceted (both OT and NT respectively) and contemporary voice.

---

29. Ibid., 100–101.
30. Ibid., 101.

THE SCOPE AND SOURCES OF BIBLICAL THEOLOGY

Since the canonical approach removes the strongholds of the descriptive (historical) task of exegesis, and at the same time includes the perspective of the prescriptive (theological) or normative task, the context of BT4 oscillates between the academy and the church. BT4 pushes against the detachment of the Bible from church doctrine and dogma stipulated by historical criticism. As much as the historical consciousness of historical criticism was correct to demand that the beliefs and practices of ancient Israel (or early Christianity) had to be respected and understood in their own historical integrity and with historical principles, the Bible must also be interpreted as a unified text of Scripture with beliefs and practices of the church that must be respected and understood in its own ecclesial integrity and with theological principles.

Thus, unlike BT1, in which theology is determined by nothing outside of the Bible's own social location, for BT4 the social location for the theology and meaning of the Bible includes not merely the Bible's historical social location(s), but also its ecclesial social location. As Moberly explains regarding Childs's concerns:

> In particular he is critical of the assumption that it is possible to determine the meaning and assess the truth claims of the Bible in historical terms independently of the Bible's reception and interpretation within the community of faith. Childs in no way denies the historical objectivity of biblical content, nor does he deny the enormous illumination that has come from purely historical study, nor does he deny the great contribution that has been made by scholars of little or no faith.... Nonetheless, among the many possible and legitimate approaches to the Bible, Childs argues that it is an approach from within the community of faith that should have normative status.[31]

Why is the community of faith the bearer of the normative status? Because there is no neutral ground on which one may stand. "The modern interpreter is no less historically-conditioned and culturally-relative in outlook than any ancient biblical writer, and must therefore stand within one or other particular context of meaning and understanding."[32] Even more, and in stark contrast to BT1, "since all interpretation involves a degree of interaction between text and reader, there is no absolute distinction between

---

31. R. W. L. Moberly, "The Church's Use of the Bible: The Work of Brevard Childs," *ExpTim* 99 (1988): 104–9 (105).
32. Ibid.

what a text meant and what a text means. The historical and evaluative tasks are inseparable."[33]

The scope of the Bible is, in the end, its subject matter—Jesus Christ. Christ is of central importance not merely to the first-century historian, but also to the church throughout the ages; not merely to the NT, but also to the OT (cf. Luke 24). Again, this is not to deny a ruled reading (e.g., Rule of Faith), for with the canonical approach even the OT is guarded against a totalizing reading of the NT that eclipses its own idiom.[34]

With this broadly defined but ecclesially normative scope, the sources of biblical theology include all the historical-critical tools of the university set within the framework and guidance of the community of faith (the church). With the community of faith as the primary social context for BT4, the source for BT4 is the canon, the sacred and authoritative Scripture for the Christian church. The canonical approach's interest in the canon is in no way narrowed to include only the final stage of the literary history of the Bible, which Sanders describes as a limitation enforced by historical criticism's inability to manage the concept of canon in any other terms.[35] Rather, the canon contains within itself the very progressive interaction between text and reader that is sought after by the contemporary church.

Several points make this clear. First, it has become increasingly clear that the canonical process was not simply postapostolic, but began within the NT itself. The NT did not just appear, but was forged out of its own living heritage of message, oral tradition, and situational proclamation. The final form of the canon is the end of a long process of progression and development.

Second, by understanding the canon to have been a progression, a simplistic picture of original author and his composition must be rejected. "Rather, the complexity of the process has emerged in which the shape of the material has been greatly affected by the circle of tradents [i.e., those who deliver something to another] to which the literature was addressed and by whom the tradition was transmitted."[36] For example, the multilayered quality of the Gospels demonstrates the active participation of the community of faith for whom the literature had a variety of religious functions in a variety of situations.[37]

---

33. Ibid.
34. See Seitz, *The Character of Christian Scripture*, 195–96.
35. Sanders, *From Sacred Story to Sacred Text*, 80–81.
36. Brevard S. Childs, *The New Testament as Canon: An Introduction* (Philadelphia: Fortress, 1985), 14.
37. As Childs (ibid., 14) explains: "the multi-layered state of the literature indicates that the process of ordering and collecting left a profound and deep stamp on the material. Again, the process of canonical shaping stood in close theological continuity with the original kerygmatic intention of the New Testament writers to use their mediums as a means of proclaiming the gospel and not to preserve an archive of historical records."

Thus, third, the theological nature of the NT continues to push back against simple historical or sociological solutions. This theological nature is defined and confined to the canon.

The source, therefore, of the canonical approach to biblical theology is nothing other than the Bible itself. This needs to be defined carefully. BT1, for example, also claimed to be the most biblical, holding in principle to the Bible only and no external traditions. In practice, however, BT1's true source is the literary, historical, and social milieu of the Bible's original context. BT4 would repudiate such a subordinating role of the Bible to historical reconstruction, while at the same time applying many of the same historical-critical tools. How so? Quite simply, while BT1 applies historical criticism *externally* to the Bible, BT4 does so only at the *internal* level of the text, that is, only to determine and diagnose the internal traditions and developments visible in the Scriptures. The source can, therefore, assume and apply numerous theological categories affirmed by the church, as long as they are internal to the text—that is, as long as they are biblical. Even more, the source for biblical theology is no longer merely the first century (for the NT) or ancient Israel (for the OT), but any and every context in which biblical ideas and categories internal to the text were applied.

In this way the canon serves as the source of biblical theology and as the context for biblical interpretation. "The status of canonicity is not an objectively demonstrable claim but a statement of Christian belief."[38] The dynamic nature of canon depicts the application of the Bible to various situations in the past and guides the contemporary interpreter in making normative (e.g., "ruled") and not merely illustrative prescriptions for the church today.

THE HERMENEUTICAL APPROACH OF BIBLICAL THEOLOGY

BT4 attempts to determine, as objectively as possible, the theology of the Bible in its canonical form. The hermeneutics of BT4 is governed by canonical parameters. The final form of the canon only served to establish a fixed context for understanding both its overall message (the gospel) as well as its constituent parts. The hermeneutics of the canonical approach to biblical theology is about reading the canon well. But as Sanders points out, "The true shape of the Bible as canon consists of its unrecorded hermeneutics which lie between the lines of most of its literature."[39] Such a hermeneutic begins with

---

38. Brevard S. Childs, *Biblical Theology in Crisis* (Philadelphia: Westminster, 1970), 99.
39. Sanders, *Canon and Community*, 46.

some of the definitions stated above: a broadly defined and developmental definition of "canon" (i.e., how the original written form was adjusted and developed over time) and a definition of "Scripture" that assumes its inspired and revelatory nature.

A canonical hermeneutic begins with the canonical form of the text. In a real way, the canonical form is the place where interpretation begins and ends; the text's prehistory and posthistory are subordinated to the text itself.[40] Ultimately the canonical reader looks for the canonical shaping internal to the text, determining the traditional material received, adapted, and promoted, leading to the intracanonical subject matter to which the entire canon witnesses. Thus, it is not just what the text says (final form), but what the text first said (first/original form) and what it has been saying (various forms between first and final).

The exploration of the canonical shape begins with a reading that looks for traces either of how the author intended the material to be understood, or the effect that a particular rendering has on the literature. The canonical intention (e.g., how the text bears traces of meaning from first to final form) becomes primary, not the author's intention (e.g., the original, historical author), for at times the canonical text receives a meaning that is derived from its function with the larger canon, "but which cannot be directly linked to the intention of an original author."[41] The canonical approach, though aware of historical forces behind the text, minimizes hidden historical references omitted by the biblical author. The present form of the text and its rendered (i.e., editorial) emphases alone provide the interpretive handles for grasping textual meaning.[42]

The canonical shape is not only within a particular passage or book, but between them. This is seen most directly in the innate relationship between the OT and NT.[43] Both testaments belong to the church and witness to the gospel of Jesus Christ. As Sheppard explains regarding a canonical hermeneutic: "By its very nature this interpretation assumes the same Word of God lies behind all parts of a book or all books in a collection, when historically

---

40. Childs, *The New Testament as Canon*, 48.

41. Ibid., 49.

42. It is important to reemphasize that this is not a slight on historical criticism, but a concern that historical criticism has for too long been the horse pulling the cart and not a tool that belongs inside the cart. The canonical approach uses historical criticism in order to read the traditions and their forces visible within the text, not the traditions connected to the text only by reconstruction and hypothetical application.

43. See Sheppard, "Canonical Criticism," 864–65, for examples of canonical connections within the traditions.

neither the parts nor the books may have been written with such a consensus of meaning in the mind of ancient authors and redactors."[44] The goal of the canonical approach is "to illuminate the writings which have been and continue to be received as authoritative by the community of faith."[45]

In the end a canonical hermeneutic requires the skill of a mechanic who, though aware in theory of an original, factory engine, is never dealing with an original engine in a used car, but only with the work and parts of several different mechanical hands, each with different approaches to making the parts of an engine work as a whole. Without ignoring the original, the mechanic works with the car as it currently exists, make-shift parts and all, in order to understand how the car is to drive in the present. There is no need to speak of the original factory model, for the only car in view is the used one standing before them. And all of the work done to it since it left the factory is now more important to the drivability of the car—and to the mechanic now working on it—than the original, factory version.

In this sense each of the previous repairs tell a story that now make the car what it is in its present, driving form. It is this repair history that becomes a (hermeneutical) guide to any future mechanic and repair. In the same way, for the canonical approach the Bible is no longer a factory original but a used vehicle that tells its own used (pre-owned) history, a history told by skilled editors (mechanics) who have added their own versions to the existing story that the Bible spoke in their past era (repairs), which now must be included if the message it speaks is to be given a voice (i.e., driven) in the present.

THE SUBJECT MATTER OF BIBLICAL THEOLOGY

A major part of the critique of historical criticism by the canonical approach is in regard to the subject matter it yields from the text. The canonical approach is convinced that a true reading of the Bible should come from the Bible itself, and that even the distinct parts of the Bible speak to the same thing. According to Sheppard, the hermeneutical method for both Judaism and Christianity involved using a "hermeneutical construct" to denote the subject matter of Scripture.[46] While *Torah* had a hermeneutical function for a Jewish reading of the OT, *Gospel* (e.g., the Rule of Faith) has a hermeneutical function for

---

44. Gerald T. Sheppard, "Canonization: Hearing the Voice of the Same God through Historically Dissimilar Traditions," *Int* 37 (1982): 21–33 (23).
45. Childs, *The New Testament as Canon*, 48.
46. Sheppard, "Canonization," 29.

Christians.[47] This hermeneutical construct defined the vision people had of the text, a vision that "assigned a common literary function to unharmonized and historically dissimilar traditions."[48]

For this reason the starting point is central for the canonical approach, since it guides what the biblical theologian is looking for. Contrary to the traditional historical-critical methodologies, Childs is convinced that "the materials for theological reflection are not the events or experiences behind the text, or apart from the construal in scripture by a community of faith and practice."[49] Rather, the biblical theologian must be concerned with theological reflection "which moves from a description of the biblical witness to the object toward which these witnesses point, that is, to their subject matter [or] substance."[50] Childs, for example, admits that this topic must avoid pitfalls of the past, as in the complexity of "substance" in theological studies and philosophical traditions, or the difficult relation of "reality" to the biblical texts in biblical studies. Yet the topic cannot be avoided, for all biblical theologies are dependent on a subject matter for its theological reflection.[51]

The subject matter of the Bible is to be found by means of an appropriate hermeneutic. Childs provides two premises on which his interpretive method moves from witness to subject matter. First, the task of exegesis involves both "explanation" and "understanding." Exegesis is a descriptive task that involves hearing each biblical text in its own integrity, but the exegetical task cannot be limited to mere description. "Explanation" and "understanding" are not two separate and distinct stages, "but two parts of the one enterprise which remain dialogically related."[52] This is a complexity that is central to the exegetical enterprise.

Second, a further complexity arises when a biblical text is subsequently interpreted within a literary framework that has the effect of reinterpreting the text in a manner different from its original meaning. "In other words, a later redactor has interpreted the text according to a different referent, that is, according to another understanding of its reality."[53] Thus, exegesis involves an analysis of both levels of a text's witness, as well as the effect of the redacted text on its understanding of the referent(s). Thus, the movement from witness to subject matter is founded on an exegetical procedure that

47. Ibid., 26.
48. Ibid., 29.
49. Brevard S. Childs, *Old Testament Theology in a Canonical Context* (Philadelphia: Fortress, 1985), 6.
50. Childs, *Biblical Theology of the Old and New Testaments*, 80.
51. For examples see ibid., 81–82.
52. Ibid., 83.
53. Ibid., 84.

pays careful attention to a text's original witness and context, but also the text's subsequent reinterpretation in new contexts.

While Childs speaks of the subject matter of the Bible as Jesus Christ, Sanders presses this identification in a different manner. Wanting to avoid asserting Jesus anachronistically in the OT, so as not "to dehistoricize Jesus and to deal with the centrality of his person in an exclusively mythological or theological manner," Sanders extends the meaning of the name of "Jesus" to "salvation."[54] To speak this way, Sanders argues, is to speak of the Bible as a canonical document, functioning in believing communities to assist in their questions of identity and purpose. Ultimately what is significant for the canonical approach is the discovery of the subject matter of the Bible that is signified and yet extends beyond the original sense and meaning of the text, especially the OT. As the book of the community of faith, the Bible is not primarily a historical document, even if it is full of historical fact; the message of the Bible is not merely an original, historical meaning, but one that transcends any one social-historical location and is applicable to the church's identity and purpose in the world at all times and in all places.

CONCLUSION

The fourth type of biblical theology, "Biblical Theology as Canonical Approach," seeks a theology of the Bible in canonical terms and based on a canonical context. Rather than being confined to external criteria and hypothetical historical reconstructions, BT4 remains committed to an authority of the Bible that is located within the Bible by means of the exegetical form and function of the canon. Proponents of a canonical approach claim that only a canonical biblical theology can hold together both the descriptive (historical) and prescriptive (theological) nature of Scripture intended for the confessing church. The Bible is the context out of which its theology is derived—and not only derived, but lived.

---

54. Sanders, *From Sacred Story to Sacred Text*, 46–47.

Chapter 8

BIBLICAL THEOLOGY AS CANONICAL APPROACH: BREVARD CHILDS

No scholar is more closely associated with a canonical approach to biblical theology than Brevard Childs (1923–2007). Born in Columbia, South Carolina, but raised primarily in New York, he was drafted into the US Army in 1942 after a year at Queens College. While being demobilized in 1945, he completed enough correspondence courses to graduate from the University of Michigan in 1947. After being raised in a home in which the Presbyterian Church exerted considerable influence on him, "it took [him] several years to get beyond Hodge and Warfield."[1] It was as a graduate student at Princeton, ironically, where he finally shed the Presbyterianism of his youth.

After graduating from Princeton with a BDiv in 1950, Childs spent four formative years in Europe as a doctoral student of OT under Eichrodt and Baumgartner at the University of Basel, Switzerland, with a beneficial term with Gerhard von Rod, the celebrated OT Scholar at Heidelberg. It was only after returning home that Childs had an influential encounter with the most noted Basel theologian, Karl Barth, an influence that came later and only through his writings. Childs served as Sterling Professor of Divinity at Yale University for just over forty years until his retirement in 1999.

As much as Childs was a student of the OT, his most important contribution is his research in biblical theology. He first addressed the problems

---

1. Quotation is taken from Roy A. Harrisville and Walter Sundberg, *The Bible in Modern Culture: Baruch Spinoza to Brevard Childs*, (2nd ed., Grand Rapids: Eerdmans, 2002), 310.

(and promise) of biblical theology in 1970 in *Biblical Theology in Crisis*. In this foundational work Childs surveys the Biblical Theology Movement, a resurgence of interest in biblical theology following the Second World War, primarily in America but in response to certain European influences, that intended to move beyond the theological impasse of the past (liberal-conservative controversy) by "accepting Biblical criticism without reservation as a valid tool while at the same time recovering a robust, confessionally oriented theology."[2] While the Biblical Theology Movement was in no way monolithic, it consisted of several general characteristics: (1) the rediscovery of the theological dimension of the Bible; (2) the unity of the whole Bible; and (3) the revelation of God in history. The most significant aspect of the Biblical Theology Movement for Childs was not what it attempted to accomplish, but what it failed to accomplish.

THE FAILURE OF CONTEMPORARY BIBLICAL THEOLOGY

According to Childs, as much as biblical theology was intending to get beyond the impasse of the previous generation, it was ultimately unable to do so. For example, although the movement had attempted to "modify the liberal insistence that the historical context was the only legitimate perspective for modern objective exegesis," the result was that "no clear alternative had emerged ... regarding the question of the context or the subject matter of the interpretation."[3] The uncertainty was felt in the exegetical results. As Childs laments, "It remains a puzzlement that Biblical Theology and exegesis did not establish a better union."[4] The methodological manhood was unequally matched with an exegetical adolescence.

Even more, the results of the Biblical Theology Movement were only felt in biblical studies; its own expectation to provide the foundation and critical norms for all theology became entirely illusionary. Ultimately, rather than opening up the Bible for the modern world, the Bible was deemed readable only when understood in its ancient, historical context. How could the God known in his great acts to the people of old be made known to the people of today?

For Childs, the Biblical Theology Movement imploded upon itself, primarily because it failed to address and was unable to answer the most crucial

---

2. Childs, *Biblical Theology in Crisis*, 21.
3. Ibid., 52.
4. Ibid., 54.

questions. What was needed was a new biblical theology, one in which questions are addressed "that not only are compatible to the Biblical material but relate to the theological task as well."[5] The first step in laying a foundation for a new biblical theology, according to Childs, is to establish the proper "context" for interpreting the Bible. By "context" Childs means the environment of that in which the Bible is being interpreted. Although the Bible has numerous interpretive contexts, including the individual contexts of both Testaments, one can still speak of *the* context of the Bible.

> The interpretation of the material will vary in relation to the particular context in which it is placed. Because there is often an interrelation between different contexts, one can expect to find areas that reflect a common design for several different contexts. The search to discover the original historical contexts ... is essential for a number of historicocritical disciplines.... However, it is also true ... that an interpreter can approach the same material and use only the final stage of the literature as a legitimate context.[6]

The context that can address both historical and theological tasks as well as discover the original historical contexts and final context is the canon. For Childs, the canon is *the* context for biblical theology. The multifaceted dimension of the canon of the Bible becomes the most ideal context for interpreting the Bible with both historical and theological sensibilities.

THE CANONICAL APPROACH TO A THEOLOGY OF THE BIBLE

Childs understands "canon" to have a historical and a theological dimension. Both aspects have a voice — a witness — that only when taken together can provide the context for biblical theology. The formation of the canon of the OT, for example, developed in a historical process, and some of its aspects and nature can be accurately described by the historian. At the same time, however, the formation of the canon of the OT also involved a "process of theological reflection within Israel arising from the impact which certain writings continued to exert upon the community through their religious use."[7] A similar formation took place in the NT. Thus, as Childs summarizes:

---

5. Ibid., 93.
6. Ibid., 98.
7. Childs, *Introduction to the Old Testament as Scripture*, 58.

The lengthy process of the development of the literature leading up to the final stage of canonization involved a profoundly hermeneutical activity on the part of the tradents. The material was transmitted through its various oral, literary, and redactional stages by many different groups toward a theological end. Because the tradents were received as religiously authoritative, they were transmitted in such a way as to maintain a normative function for subsequent generations of believers within a community of faith. The process of rendering the material theologically involved countless different compositional techniques by means of which the tradition was actualized.[8]

Thus, when Childs uses the term "canonical," it is being used as a cipher to encompass the above-stated formation of the literature.

In its parts Childs's use of the term "canon" denotes (1) the reception and acknowledgment of the literature as authoritative, (2) the process by which the collection arose leading up to its final stage of stabilization, and (3) the theological (canonical) extension of the texts' primary meaning(s). In this way the historical and theological aspects of the Bible coalesce.

For the biblical theologian, therefore, the theological function of the canon "lies in its affirmation that the authoritative norm lies in the literature itself as it has been treasured, transmitted, and transformed ... and not in 'objectively' reconstructed stages of the process."[9] This canonical process is not a dogmatic decision imposed on certain texts, nor is it only a consideration of the final form of the canon. Rather, the canonical approach, for Childs, involves not only the entire Christian canon—both Testaments— but it also involves the entire history of the canon, including all the textual processes and people of faith involved. The text reveals a history of its own "active shaping"—a canonical shaping—in which each generation faithfully received and intentionally transmitted the material, "rendering the tradition accessible to the future generations by means of a 'canonical intentionality,' which is coextensive with the meaning of the biblical text."[10] Stated more simply and using the analogy we used in the previous chapter, both the original and repaired parts of the engine (i.e., the edited elements) work together to make the car drive (i.e., determine the meaning of the text) for today.

The canonical approach, therefore, combines not only the historical with the theological, but also the past with the present. Not only is this, according to Childs, the most comprehensive context in which to place the Bible, but it is also the most natural—in the sense that it is neither imposing an ancient

---

8. Childs, *Biblical Theology of the Old and New Testaments*, 70.
9. Ibid., 71.
10. Childs, *Introduction to the Old Testament as Scripture*, 78–79.

(historical) context on a modern text, nor imposing a modern (theological) context on an ancient text, but is able to handle both in a collaborative fashion. Even more, rather than imposing anything on the text, the canonical approach is drawing the developing formulation from the text itself. As Childs explains regarding the canonical approach:

> It is built into the structure of the text itself.... The modern hermeneutical impasse which has found itself unable successfully to bridge the gap between the past and the present, has arisen in large measure from its disregard of the canonical shaping. The usual critical method of biblical exegesis is, first, to seek to restore an original historical setting by stripping away those very elements which constitute the canonical shape. Little wonder that once the biblical text has been securely anchored in the historical past by "decanonizing" it, the interpreter has difficulty applying it to the modern religious context.[11]

Childs was adamant that this was not a criticism (contra Sanders), nor even a method, but a manner of reading the Bible.[12] Unfortunately, Childs's all-inclusive approach was at best hardly understood, and at worst warped and abused.[13] We have given an overview of Childs's canonical approach, but in order to explain it further we must address some of its essential parts.

THE LITERAL SENSE OF SCRIPTURE

The problem for biblical theology is what Childs calls "a tale of two testaments."[14] As Childs explains:

> Up to now the emphasis for reconstituting Biblical Theology has fallen on the need for such an enterprise of biblical interpretation to hear the different voices of both Testaments in their canonical integrity. Yet a fundamental problem immediately emerges when the New Testament's use of the Old Testament cannot be easily reconciled with the Old Testament's own witness.[15]

---

11. Ibid., 79.
12. Childs did not prefer the title "canonical criticism" because he saw the canon approach as something different than another criticism, as in the next step on from redaction criticism. Childs's use of canon was to establish a context and perspective for interpretation, within which all existing methods and tools can be appropriately exercised.
13. For a full evaluation of some of the confusion surrounding Childs's canonical approach and method, see Daniel R. Driver, *Brevard Childs, Biblical Theologian* (Forschungen zum Alten Testament 2.46; Tübingen: Mohr Siebeck, 2010).
14. Brevard S. Childs, "A Tale of Two Testaments," *Int* 26 (1972): 20–29. This article is an extended book review of Hans-Joachim Kraus, *Die Biblische Theologie: Ihre Geschichte und Problematik* (Neukirchen-Vluyn: Neukirchen Verlag, 1970).
15. Childs, *Biblical Theology of the Old and New Testaments*, 80.

This problem cannot be resolved by harmonizing the differences, by subordinating the OT to the NT, or by an appeal to some form of "salvation history." Since the problem is in regard to the "literal sense" of the text, or its plain sense, the problem must be resolved at the level of the literal sense of Scripture. Stated as a question: How does the interpreter move from the literal sense of the text to its subject matter?

Since, for Childs, the true subject matter of the Bible is Jesus Christ, it is important for him to define what exactly the "literal sense" of the Bible is, especially as one reads the OT. The subject matter is intimately tied to the literal sense of the text, but in a literal sense that is not merely historical, the "original" sense, but also theological, the "redacted" sense or the developing, contemporary sense. As Childs explains, "a fundamental characteristic of the [historical] critical movement was its total commitment to the literal sense of the text."[16]

> The historical sense of the text was construed as being the *original* meaning of the text as it emerged in its pristine situation. Therefore, the aim of the interpreter was to reconstruct the original occasion of the historical reference on the basis of which the truth of the biblical text could be determined. In sum, the *sensus literalis* [literal sense] had become the *sensus originalis* [original sense].[17]

For Childs, the identification of the literal sense with the historical sense has had four negative consequences.[18] First, any claim for the integrity of the literal sense is virtually destroyed. The explanation of the text is now governed by historical research; the literal sense merely provides a way behind the text to some historical reality. Second, the task of biblical interpretation becomes a highly speculative enterprise. The literal sense dissolves before the hypothetical reconstructions of the original situations on whose recovery correct interpretation ultimately depends. Third, the concept of the Bible as the Scripture of a community of faith has been sharply altered. Fourth, the religious use of the Bible is challenged because of the insurmountable gap that has arisen between the historical sense of the text, now fully anchored in the historical past, and the search of its present relevance for the modern age. This fourth consequence, it is interesting to note, is commonly referred

---

16. Brevard S. Childs, "The *Sensus Literalis* of Scripture: An Ancient and Modern Problem," in *Beiträge zur Alttestamentlichen Theologie: Festschrift für Walter Zimmerli zum 70. Geburtstag* (ed. Herbert Donner, Robert Hanhart, and Rudolf Smend; Göttingen: Vandenhoeck & Ruprecht, 1977), 80–93 (88).
17. Ibid., 89.
18. The following is adapted from ibid., 90–91.

to today as the unavoidable impasse between "what it meant" and "what it means" (e.g., BT1).

Childs's response is clear: "to restrict biblical interpretation to a strictly grammatical reading seemed to threaten the whole theological dimension of the Bible."[19] The object of biblical exegesis is the text itself and the subject matter about which the text speaks — something for Childs that includes the message of the canon as a whole (Genesis to Revelation) with all of its editorial development. The study of the text simply cannot be separated from its reality. Even more, for Childs the study of the biblical text must be closely connected with the community of faith that treasured it. It is only sacred Scripture in a context of faith. As Childs explains:

> The literal sense of the text is the plain sense witnessed to by the community of faith. It makes no claim of being the original sense, or even being the best. Rather, *the literal sense of the canonical Scriptures offers a critical theological norm for the community of faith on how the tradition functions authoritatively for future generations of the faithful.*[20]

Thus, for Childs, there can be no genuine "literal sense" apart from a commitment to canon. The literal sense "was never restricted to a verbal, philological exercise alone, but functioned ... as a 'ruled reading' in which a balance was struck between a grammatical reading and the structure of communal practice or a 'rule of faith.'"[21]

The subject matter of the Bible, therefore, is to be found in "the relation between the historical study of the Bible and its theological use as religious literature."[22] The subject matter is not merely the original, historical referent, though it is certainly not less. The subject matter includes simultaneously a further level that does not in any way contradict the literal/historical reading, but rather extends it. In Childs's own words: "This reading emerges from the recognition of a two part canon and it seeks to analyze structural similarities and dissimilarities between the witnesses of both Testaments, Old and New."[23] This approach is neither a history-of-religions comparison of two sets of writings, nor is it a merely descriptive history of exegesis. Rather, "it is an exegetical and theological enterprise which seeks to pursue a relationship of content.... A level of theological construction is brought together in rigorous

---

19. Ibid., 87.
20. Ibid., 92 (emphasis added).
21. Childs, "Toward Recovering Theological Exegesis," 126.
22. Childs, "Response to Reviewers of *Introduction to the Old Testament as Scripture*," 58.
23. Childs, "Does the Old Testament Witness to Jesus Christ?" 61.

reflection in which the full reality of the subject matter of Scripture, gained from a close hearing of each separate testament, is explored."[24] Thus:

> At the heart of the Christian faith lies an apparent paradox in relation to two Scriptures. On the one hand, its canonical form which consists of two Testaments provides a warrant for respecting two discrete voices according to the literal/plain sense of the texts. On the other hand, the Christian Church affirms that its Christian Bible is a unified witness bearing testimony to one Lord, Jesus Christ, who is the divine reality underlying the entire biblical canon.[25]

Jesus Christ, according to Childs, is the subject matter or substance of the Christian, two-Testament Bible.

THE THEOLOGICAL TASK OF BIBLICAL THEOLOGY

The hermeneutical role of biblical theology is to understand the various voices within the whole Christian Bible, both OT and NT, as witnesses to Jesus Christ. The OT "bears testimony to the Christ who has not yet come; the New to the Christ who has appeared in the fullness of time."[26] The relation between the Testaments, however, moves beyond the level of their witnesses, for to remain on the textual level is "to miss the key which unites dissident voices into a harmonious whole. Rather, Biblical Theology attempts to hear the different voices in relation to the divine reality to which they point in such diverse ways."[27] Though in different ways, at different times, and to different people, both Testaments bear witness to the one Lord, and it is the theological task of biblical theology to allow them all rightly to be heard and understood.

This theological task is not timeless and speculative, but is concerned with "concrete historical communities ... who are trying to be faithful in their own particular historical contexts."[28] Yet the different contexts, even different Testaments, are not being faithful to their own identity, to themselves, but to that to which they point: Jesus Christ. Thus, even in the OT, Jesus is implicitly the subject matter, and this is in no way an imposition. The move from witness to reality requires "the specific biblical theological task of *pursuing*

---

24. Ibid., 61–62.
25. Childs, "Toward Recovering Theological Exegesis," 125.
26. Childs, *Biblical Theology of the Old and New Testaments*, 85.
27. Ibid.
28. Ibid., 86.

theologically the nature of this reality throughout the entire Christian canon."[29] The movement from witness to reality, therefore, also goes in reverse direction, as the reality explains and informs the nature of the witness.

This is not an attempt to read the OT in light of the NT, thus giving the OT text its "proper interpretation," for such a hermeneutic not only demands that Jesus Christ was the literal sense subject of the OT, but it also completely undercuts the continuing canonical role of the OT as Christian Scripture. In contrast, the theological task of biblical theology is to allow the biblical language naturally "to resonate in a new and creative fashion when read from the vantage point of a fuller understanding of Christian truth. Such a reading is not intended to threaten the [literal sense] of the text, but *to extend through figuration a reality which has been only partially heard."*[30]

BIBLICAL THEOLOGY AS A MULTI-LEVEL APPROACH

The theological task, therefore, combines and interrelates exegesis and dogmatics. Childs describes the activity as a "multi-level interpretation" and provides a three-step process.

The Literal or Plain Sense: Beginning with the Ancient Text

In order to hear the voice of the OT's witness in its own right, it is necessary to interpret each passage within its historical, literary, and canonical context. One must deal seriously with the OT genre of story as a legitimate form of witness, and one must not read back into the story the person of Jesus or interpret various theophanies of the second person of the Trinity. Such impositions distort the OT witness and eclipse its voice. It is essential that the move from witness to reality strives "to relate the text's verbal sense to the theological reality which confronted historic Israel in evoking this witness."[31]

The Extended or Figurative Sense: Dialogue between Ancient Text and Canon

The second avenue into the Christian Bible does not in itself contradict the literal/historical reading but rather extends it. This extended reading "emerges from the recognition of a two part canon and it seeks to analyze structural similarities and dissimilarities between the witnesses of both Testaments."[32] This is

---

29. Ibid., 87 (emphasis added).
30. Ibid. (emphasis added).
31. Childs, "Does the Old Testament Witness to Jesus Christ?" 61.
32. Ibid.

not a history-of-religions comparison or merely a descriptive history of exegesis; rather, it is an exegetical and theological enterprise, which pursues "a relationship of content." Taking, for example, an understanding of God, this second avenue explores the features the two Testaments hold in common respecting the mode, intention, and goal of God's manifestations. This is not a comparison merely on the cultural level. Instead, a theological enterprise is engaged in which neither witness is absorbed by the other, nor are their contents fused. "A theological relationship is pursued both on the level of the textual witness and on that of the discrete [subject] matter ... of the two collections."[33]

The Constructed or Canonical Sense: Dialogue between Subject Matter and Ancient Text

The third avenue to biblical exegesis arises from the Christian confession that the church's Bible comprises a theological unity although its form combines two distinct sections, each with a unique voice. "The pursuit of the nature of this theological relationship provides the focus toward engaging critically this dimension of exegesis."[34] A level of theological construction is brought together in rigorous reflection in which the full reality of the subject matter of Scripture, gained from a close reading of each distinct Testament, is explored. The interpreter now proceeds in a direction that moves from the reality itself back to the textual witness. The biblical text in its canonical form "exerts theological pressure" on the reader, which demands that the two witnesses be critically united.

This multi-level interpretive approach, extending itself to the different dimensions of the Christian Bible, is still a single method. Each of the "senses" is to be understood as relating to one another. There is no necessary linear order, even though Childs presents the "steps" in a sequential fashion. This single method, however, is complex enough to engage the historical and theological levels of the Bible. Returning to the example of an understanding of God, how might the church's trinitarian formulation be understood exegetically? According to Childs, it is incorrect to suggest that the church merely introduced Greek speculation into a Hebrew tradition. This entirely misunderstands the church's response to the witness of Scripture. "The one God of both Testaments is surely monotheistic, but not a monad; rather, God is a dynamic divine reality in constant inner-communication."[35] In a similar manner, to speak of Jesus Christ as the subject matter of the Bible

---

33. Ibid. 62.
34. Ibid.
35. Ibid.

is to move beyond the task of hearing the unique voice of the prophets' testimony to a coming royal figure. Rather, in the light of the life, death, and resurrection of Jesus Christ in the history of Israel, the texts of both Testaments in their fragmentary testimony to God's utterly mysterious purpose of new creation and redemption take on fresh life. Thus, when the interpreter moves from the reality of God manifest in action back to the Scriptures themselves for further illumination, he or she is *constrained to listen for a new song to break forth from the same ancient, sacred texts.*[36]

For this very reason a multi-level interpretation is required, in order to be able to handle the full range of the different functions and contexts of Scripture.

The biblical theology of Brevard Childs cannot merely be described as a method or approach, but as a way of positioning oneself to the Bible. The nature of the position is rooted in the demands of reading the Bible within the church and in relation to God. Childs's method "is an interpretive stance or orientation that seeks to interpret the Bible as sacred Scripture within communities of faith, guided by the Holy Spirit, who continues to speak new words from God through Scripture in each generation. Childs's canonical approach is not just another method or criticism but more of a posture."[37] That the Bible still speaks and that the church still listens and responds are rooted in the fact that the living God is the ultimate reality behind biblical theology. As Childs himself explains, the goal of biblical theology is to instruct the reader of the Bible "toward an understanding of God that leads from faith to faith."[38]

ASSESSMENT

In the end, for Childs biblical theology is an enterprise that is both historical and theological. In fact, the relation between them is of vital importance. Rather than conceiving of a competitive approach, pitting history and theology against one another, or a developmental approach, moving in a linear fashion from history to theology, Childs conceives a relation between history and theology that is circular, even helical, so that each one informs and counter-informs the other. The locus of authority that can handle both history and theology is the canon, which for Childs is necessary to sustain the life of biblical theology. Childs put the canon on the map in reference to hermeneutics and theology.

Childs's use of canon was forced on him by the pressure exerted from both authoritative sides of the biblical-theological task: history with its literal

---

36. Ibid., 62–63 (emphasis added).
37. Dennis T. Olson, "Seeking 'the Inexpressible Texture of Thy Word': A Practical Guide to Brevard Childs' Canonical Approach to Theological Exegesis," *PTR* 14 (2008): 53–68 (55).
38. Childs, *Biblical Theology of the Old and New Testaments*, 382.

sense on the one side and theology with its ultimate subject matter on the other. Only by traveling by means of the canon could the interpreter and biblical theologian avoid distorting one of the two authorities, each having their own integrity and legitimate concerns. As much as Childs is known for his canonical approach, his attempt to relate exegesis and dogmatics is probably his greatest contribution.[39] Yet it is his canonical legacy that is the source of much attention, as well as much confusion. Childs's use of "canon" was complex, and his canonical "posture" for a method caused many to raise questions. A few confusions or concerns can briefly be addressed.[40]

The greatest area of confusion, and not without warrant, is Childs's use of the term "canon" or "canonical." Moberly argues that the term is less important than is sometimes supposed.[41] Not only does Childs use the terminology in a varied manner, but it also is more fittingly understood as convenient shorthand for his entire approach to the Bible as authoritative Scripture for the community of faith. The confusion is not only in regard to the term in a general sense, but also the exact function of the dynamic "canon." The fundamentally different accounts of "canon," especially the open or closed nature of the OT canon by the time of the early church, causes confusion and disagreement from the moment the term is spoken.[42]

Moreover, even if one agrees in principle to some sort of "canonical consciousness," what does that actually look like? Although many conservatives supported his focus on the final form of the canon, for Childs the canon — that is, the canonical development visible within the final form of the canon — was important from start to finish. But can the canon's history and tradents be located and defined in a manner suggested by Childs? Has he, as Ian Provan suggests, vastly underestimated the level of intertextuality in the final form of the OT only to recover an intertextuality at the earlier stages of the tradition, relying more heavily on traditional historical-critical exegesis than any other kinds of textual reading?[43] Even more, has Childs critiqued historical reconstruction behind the text only to pick it up again at the level of the canonical tradents? Such questions not only reveal the histori-

---

39. It is also worth mentioning that Childs is one of the only biblical theologians in recent years who has written a biblical theology on the whole Bible.

40. For a full evaluation of critiques and a response, see Driver, *Brevard Childs, Biblical Theologian*.

41. Moberly, "The Church's Use of the Bible," 108.

42. For a summary of this debate in the context of Childs's canonical approach see Stephen Dempster, "Canons on the Right and Canons on the Left: Finding a Resolution in the Canon Debate," *JETS* 52 (2009): 47–77.

43. Iain Provan, "Canons to the Left of Him: Brevard Childs, His Critics, and the Future of Old Testament Theology," *SJT* 50 (1997): 1–38 (29).

cal and hermeneutical complexity of the canonical approach, but also serve to challenge some of its methodological foundations.

Another criticism refers to the relation Childs posits between history and theology. Can an approach based necessarily on the conclusions of the last two centuries of historical criticism shift so easily to a theological reading and recovery of the Bible's subject matter? The historical critic works emphatically with the human author, whereas the theologian works more unashamedly with the divine author and the church. Can the subject matter of one be so smoothly passed on to the other? By taking his foundational cues *within* the text but establishing the ultimate meaning by means of an authority *outside* the text, Childs may be functioning, as Dale Brueggeman has suggested, as a postcritical biblicist—that is, a strange mixture of some of the tendencies of "conservatism" alongside the standard, more "liberal" appropriation of historical criticism.[44] By standing in such a position Childs guarantees that he will be neither claimed nor understood by either side of the theological spectrum.

Finally, as helpful as Childs has been to bring the Bible back within the church, his approach is not without problems. Some have argued that the exegetical function of the church for Childs subordinates the Bible to the church, which downplays the church's derivative nature: God "spoke" and "called out" the church.[45] But even if we sidestep that issue, there is still the question regarding what Childs assumes is the nature of the church's engagement with the Bible as Scripture. Childs gives little attention to the wide diversity of outlooks within the church and the apparently irresolvable problem of conflicting interpretations.[46] This concern becomes especially disconcerting when one considers the two different religious traditions (Jewish and Christian) represented by the two-Testament Bible. As helpful as the church initially appears in regards to biblical interpretation, it shortly becomes its own uncompromising handicap.[47]

---

44. Dale A. Brueggeman, "Brevard Childs' Canon Criticism: An Example of Post-Critical Naiveté," *JETS* 32 (1989): 311–26. Using Ricoeur's hermeneutical methodology of three steps or moments, Brueggman suggests Childs is in the third moment, a second naiveté.

45. Cf. C. F. H. Henry, "Canonical Theology: An Evangelical Appraisal," *SBET* 8 (1990): 76–108; John Piper, "Authority and Meaning of the Christian Canon: A Response to Gerald Sheppard on Canon Criticism," *JETS* 19 (1976): 87–96.

46. Moberly, "The Church's Use of the Bible," 108–9.

47. According to Provan, "Canons to the Left of Him," 15–16, for all the "ecumenical noises" in Childs's stated methodology, one doubts if he actually believes it. "In order for his general approach to be well-grounded, Childs is required to defend the notion of a Jewish canon (and text) which is canonical also for the church." For a critique of this sort from the perspective of BT2 see D. A. Carson, "New Testament Theology," in *Dictionary of the Later New Testament and Its Development* (ed. R. P. Martin and P. H. Davids; Downers Grove, IL: InterVarsity Press, 1997), 796–814 (804).

TYPE 5: BIBLICAL THEOLOGY AS THEOLOGICAL CONSTRUCTION

Chapter 9

BIBLICAL THEOLOGY AS THEOLOGICAL CONSTRUCTION: DEFINITION

The fifth type of biblical theology (BT5) posits a modest critique of the abuses of historical criticism and proposes a specifically theological approach to biblical theology. In contrast to compartmentalizing biblical scholars and theologians, who are not only working in isolation from each other but also in isolation from the concerns of the church, BT5 is part of a movement that is concerned to retrieve the convictions and skills that allowed previous Christians to permit scriptural interpretation to shape and be shaped by Christian principles and practices. In short, BT5 is concerned to recast the Bible from its status as an ancient, historical text to contemporary Christian Scripture.

BT5 is associated with a growing interest in a theological interpretation of Scripture.[1] With Robert Morgan we might describe the practice of this movement as "all theologically motivated interpretation," even though the actual interpretive forms can look distinct.[2] While definitions and distinctions abound, it is a fair assessment to claim that biblical theology and a "theological interpretation" can be best described as interrelated in practice even if different in form. Ultimately the family resemblances between BT5

---

1. For an introduction to this movement see Daniel J. Treier, *Introducing Theological Interpretation of Scripture: Recovering a Christian Practice* (Grand Rapids: Baker, 2008).
2. Robert Morgan, "Can Critical Study of Scripture Provide a Doctrinal Norm?" *JR* 76 (1996): 206–32 (212).

and "theological interpretation" cannot be denied, nor can the overlap in a host of specific presuppositions and methods.[3] In the least, BT5 has absorbed much of the interests of the theological interpretation movement so that its practitioners strive to position themselves outside the academy's "departmentalization" of biblical studies and systematic theology with its bifurcation between ancient text and contemporary Scripture.[4]

In light of BT5's openness to a theological approach to the Bible, a key difference is easily recognizable between BT5 and the other approaches to biblical theology: the relevance for today. BT1, for example, was committed to freeing itself from the anachronistic interpretations of its predecessors and forced itself to accept the hiatus between the time and ideas of the Bible and the time and ideas of the modern world. Thus, BT1 makes certain that history—and by "history" they imply the specific biblical history—is the sole, mediating category. Such an approach is controlled by a historical-critical methodology and is descriptive in nature.

While the other types are less descriptive than BT1, they too have their relevance mediated through less than contemporary categories (e.g., the "special history" category of BT2, the narrative category of BT3, and the canon category of BT4). In contrast, BT5, with the conviction that the Bible properly belongs to the church, is convinced that for Christians the Bible is *their* Bible, not the Bible of foreign people in a foreign time and land. "This means that Christians are called not merely to generate … scriptural interpretations but to embody those interpretations as well."[5] Such an approach is controlled by a theological methodology and a theological category that is prescriptive in nature.

THE TASK OF BIBLICAL THEOLOGY

What is central for BT5 is the integrated methodology of biblical theology, especially the relationship of biblical studies to the theological task and confession of the Christian church. While biblical theology might be something done by academics, the true home of biblical theology is in the worshiping context of the church. For BT5 its task, therefore, is a specifically *Christian* task. Stephen Fowl gives a helpful explanation of this distinction:

---

3. For a helpful reflection of overlap between biblical theology and theological interpretation of Scripture see Daniel J. Treier, "Biblical Theology and/or Theological Interpretation of Scripture?" *SJT* 61 (2008): 16–31.

4. For a critique of the "theological interpretation movement," not only in regard to the claim that historical criticism cannot be "theological" but also that the self-proclaimed title is artificially narrow, see John C. Poirier, " 'Theological Interpretation' and Its Contradistinctions," *TynBul* 61 (2010): 105–18.

5. Stephen E. Fowl, *Engaging Scripture: A Model for Theological Interpretation* (Challenges in Contemporary Theology; Malden, MA: Blackwell, 1998), 2.

To identify oneself as a Christian is, at the same time, to bring oneself into a particular sort of relationship to the Bible in which the Bible functions as a normative standard for faith and practice. For the professional biblical scholar, the Bible is simply one (among many) texts upon which scholars might bring their interpretive interests and practices to bear. Christians stand in a different relationship to the Bible. The Bible, for Christians, is their Scripture ... Scripture is authoritative.[6]

In this way the posture and presuppositions of the Christian church are given primary authority over the practice of biblical theology. Stated succinctly, *the task of BT5 is to affirm the integrated nature of biblical theology as a theological, hermeneutical, and exegetical discipline with overriding theological concerns, incorporating biblical scholarship into the larger enterprise of Christian theology.* This can be supported by several necessary explanations.

First, biblical theology is the theology of the Bible that exists in the present, not in the past. In contrast to BT1, which saw itself as something new, BT5 perceives itself to be part of something old — part of the long-standing Christian tradition. BT5 is not only concerned with the overpowering influence of historical criticism, which by its very nature is a dominating and controlling force, but also with what they deemed to be the inappropriate removal of the Bible from the church and its relocation to the university. A true reading of the Bible must be "ecclesially responsible."[7] That is to say, "a line has been drawn around this collection of writings, demarcating it from other writings that may or may not perform analogous normative functions in other communities."[8] The Bible is controlling of and controlled by its ecclesial community, its canon, and its interpretive tradition.[9]

For this reason the Bible cannot belong primarily to the academy, for before the university ever existed, it was already the property of the church. It is also

---

6. Ibid., 3.
7. Francis Watson, "Authors, Readers, Hermeneutics," in *Reading Scripture with the Church: Toward a Hermeneutic for Theological Interpretation* (ed. A. K. M. Adam et al.; Grand Rapids: Baker Academic, 2006), 119.
8. Ibid.
9. A renewed interest in theological readings of Scripture has led to a renewed interest in premodern methods and readings of Scripture as well as the Rule of Faith. According to Robert W. Wall, "Reading the Bible from within Our Traditions: The 'Rule of Faith' in Theological Hermeneutics," in *Between Two Horizons: Spanning New Testament Studies and Systematic Theology* (ed. Joel B. Green and Max Turner; Grand Rapids: Eerdmans, 2000), 88 – 107: "The Rule of Faith is the grammar of theological agreements which Christians confess to be true and by which all of Scripture is rendered in forming a truly Christian faith and life.... Though formally distinct from Scripture, the Rule of Faith formulates the church's attempt to demarcate the significance of what the Jesus of history said and did (Acts 1:1) and also to make sense of the church's ongoing experience with the living Jesus" (88 – 89).

worth adding that suggestions that attempt to claim the NT for the church and claim the OT for the Jewish community are equally abusive to the collection as a whole. To separate any part of the two-Testament Bible from the church is to do damage to the whole. That is, to read the OT as a Jewish "Scripture" is at best the complete reorientation of the reading strategy of the OT and the reciprocally shaped nature of the two-Testament Christian canon, and at worst demands that the OT writings are the sole property of the Jewish community. Whereas for the Christian the OT must be included as Christian Scripture, "scholars of the 'Hebrew Bible' need the New Testament almost as little as New Testament scholars need the Koran."[10] For BT5 the reception of some texts and not others assigns them a complex function that services only one community: the church.[11]

Second, biblical theology is a hermeneutical method for Christian Scripture, not an ancient text. For BT5 it is axiomatic that the Bible cannot be read like any other text or book. The Bible is nothing less than Holy Scripture, which is inherently and theologically unique in nature, both in ontology and function.[12] Francis Watson suggests that the best approach to the unique nature of the Bible is to consider it as its own genre: "If genre is a function of communal reception and usage as well as of inherent characteristics, then the genre of the biblical texts is that of 'holy Scripture.'"[13]

This is not to deny that there is a historical distance between the texts and the contemporary readers, nor does it deny a place for historical understanding or approaches to the text. Rather, it is to suggest that the Bible must be defined as a living text and must be interpreted within the live worship of the contemporary church. The very fact of canonization implies a confessional stance and grounds the Bible primarily in the present. The view that supposes texts are wholly limited and confined by their immediate circumstances of origin and that as soon as they stray from their appointed time and place they will be misread and misunderstood, is to embrace a historical perception of this body of writings that is theologically and communally foreign to them and their practitioners.

---

10. Francis Watson, *Text and Truth: Redefining Biblical Theology* (Grand Rapids: Eerdmans, 1997), 5.

11. This is not to deny the usefulness of the Bible in other communities like, for example, the university. According to Francis Watson, *Text, Church and World: Biblical Interpretation in Theological Perspective* (Edinburgh: T&T Clark, 1994), 7: "It is held that the secular institution is interested in these texts partly by virtue of the disinterested pursuit of truth that is its mission, partly because of their pervasive influence on western history and culture, and partly in order to counter the influence of those who allegedly misuse the texts in ways that might be socially damaging." Even biblical scholarship in the academy proceeds under the umbrella of this shared vision of secularity, which quite easily removes the theological pestilence from the historical body of writings.

12. Helpful here is D. Christopher Spinks, *The Bible and the Crisis of Meaning: Debates on the Theological Interpretation of Scripture* (London: T&T Clark, 2007), 8–17.

13. Watson, *Text, Church and World*, 227.

Third, the overriding guide and concern of biblical theology is theological. The separation of the Bible and theology is not a new phenomenon, but is the consequence of the Enlightenment project, which considered the condemnation of ecclesial and religious traditions to be a "modern" improvement.[14] As Christopher Seitz polemically states, "Having labored for two centuries to free the Bible from dogmatic overlay, Protestant and Catholic critics alike should 'concede victory.'"[15]

The growing interest in theological readings of the Bible, and therefore biblical theology, has been pressured by several factors.[16] These include (1) the substantial collapse of modernity's dream of "objectivity," with its allied dichotomy of discoverable "facts" from merely subjective "beliefs/values" (i.e., "theology"); (2) the recognition that the subject matter and implied readership of the Bible are overtly theological and religious, inviting nuanced theological reflection; (3) the understanding that from the outset the biblical writings were read "canonically," and thus that the unity of the Testaments was and remains a substantial and significant issue; and (4) the renewed emphasis on the role of the reader (in history and today), which has blurred the distinction between exegesis and interpretation and has opened up the (postmodern) way to a plethora of ideological and theological readings.

The result of this interest is the growing conviction that the Bible is characterized by a governing interest in God and that the Bible's authors, the text itself, and the original community of readers were innately theological.[17] Thus, there is no need to impose theology or theological systems on the Bible, for theology has been underlying and pressuring the nature of the Bible and its reception from the start. Ultimately for BT5, the subdiscipline of biblical *theology* places emphasis on the theological nature of the Bible.

THE USE OF BIBLICAL THEOLOGY

If the task of biblical theology for BT5 is theological in nature, the use of biblical theology is the confession of the church, in contrast to the academy. Biblical theology of this sort must incorporate and be ruled (e.g., the Rule of

---

14. Joel B. Green, "Scripture and Theology: Uniting the Two So Long Divided," in *Between Two Horizons*, 23–43 (24–25). Cf. Alister E. McGrath, *The Genesis of Doctrine: A Study in the Foundation of Doctrinal Criticism* (Grand Rapids: Eerdmans, 1990), 81.

15. Christopher R. Seitz, *Word without End: The Old Testament as Abiding Theological Witness* (Grand Rapids: Eerdmans, 1998), 15.

16. The following are adapted from Max Turner and Joel B. Green, "New Testament Commentary and Systematic Theology: Strangers or Friends?" in *Between Two Horizons*, 1–22 (8–9).

17. Cf. Kevin J. Vanhoozer, "Introduction: What is Theological Interpretation of the Bible?" in *DTIB*, 19–25.

Faith) by faith commitments, that is, theological presuppositions. This is no public discussion, for biblical theology is the sole practice of the church, the confessing community. This is not to say that such a use of biblical theology is uncritical, but only to claim that the concern is not with secular models of truth, but with in-house models defined entirely by the confessing church. It might be argued that such an agenda is even more critical than secular interests, for it is not only intending to be critical of biblical authors and biblical texts but also of contemporary readers. In this way "theological criticism" might be viewed as the most inclusive of interpretive criticisms:

> It is not that text criticism and other forms of criticism have no role; it is rather a matter of the ultimate aim of reading. Those who seek to interpret Scripture theologically want to hear the word of God in Scripture and hence to be transformed by the renewing of their minds (Rom. 12:2). In this respect, it is important to note that God must not be an "afterthought" in biblical interpretation. God is not simply a function of a certain community's interpretive interest; instead, God is prior to both the community and the biblical texts themselves. A properly theological criticism will therefore seek to do justice to the priority of God.[18]

This kind of model for conceiving of the Bible involves not only the mind but also—and necessarily so—the heart. By involving the mind and the heart, biblical theology requires a constructive and interactive application of convictions, practices, and scriptural interpretation that is particularly Christian. These convictions and shapes serve not only to define the use of biblical theology, but also to shape the habits of biblical theologian(s). "Christians need to manifest a certain form of common life if this interaction is to serve faithful life and worship."[19]

For this reason Fowl, for example, is convinced that biblical theology as normally practiced in the modern university is inappropriately equipped for such an enterprise because of the sharp division of labor that results in fragmenting disciplines each concerned with its own integrity as a discipline. The church's use of biblical theology is so consumed with not only the interpretation but also the embodiment of Scripture that even the slightest fragmenting between its parts must be deemed inappropriate by definition.[20]

In contrast then to BT1, in which a concern for the Bible removed it from the naïve influence of the church, BT5 is convinced that only in the church can

---

18. Ibid., 22.
19. Fowl, *Engaging Scripture*, 8.
20. Ibid., 13–21.

the Bible be handled by its true form and nature. Contra Stendahl, there is a hiatus between the message of the Bible and its ancient social location and the message of contemporary social locations only when that social location is not the church; only since the removal of the Bible from the vicinity of the church has there been a need for a translation of the Bible's message.[21] And contra the other types, not even a special "history" (BT2) or a special "story" (BT3) or a special "canon" (BT4) does enough to translate the Bible from its academic language into an ecclesial tongue. In short, the Bible, even with its ancient origin, is not foreign to the church, just as the God of the Bible, also ancient in origin, is not foreign to the church but is to be addressed as "our Father." If there is any translation needed, it must be done by the church, a translation provided in both word and deed to a world that is reading a very different script.

THE SCOPE AND SOURCES OF BIBLICAL THEOLOGY

With the church as the primary social location and Christian theology as the primary frame of reference, the scope and sources are derived from the theological context of the Bible as Christian Scripture. In what can be seen as a marital reconciliation after the divorce between text and tradition caused by the Enlightenment,[22] BT5 conceives of the scope and sources of biblical theology to be defined by the breadth and depth of Christian theology and its ecclesial tradition. Thus, for BT5 the scope of biblical theology can be nothing less than both OT and NT, and even then their relation cannot be in some form of never-ending conflict since they must interrelate as the two parts of the singular canon.

Defining the exact nature of the interrelation between OT and NT is clearly a matter of complex debate—as it was for the early Christians, who worked hard to provide an appropriate Christian interpretation of the OT. But to separate the first and second Testament is to do damage to both the unity of the canon and to the interrelation of its parts, for neither Testament can be appropriately read without the other. "The Old Testament adds a dimension of depth to the New, without which the New would seem thin, superficial and narrow; the New Testament gives direction and scope to the Old, without which the Old would seem unfocused, irrelevant and alien."[23]

---

21. Cf. Krister Stendahl, "Biblical Theology, Contemporary," in *IDB*, 1:430.
22. According to Watson, *Text and Truth*, 305: "The Enlightenment's radicalizing of the Reformer's disjunction of text and tradition has led to a fundamental rejection of the entire history of classical Christian interpretation of Christian canonical texts."
23. Francis Watson, "The Old Testament as Christian Scripture: A Response to Professor Seitz," *SJT* 52 (1999): 227–32.

This "living dynamic" between and across the two Testaments requires biblical theology to be rooted in a two-Testament-pressured interpretive practice.[24]

For BT5 the role of the Bible as a source is based not in relation to its historical origin and nature but its theological origin and nature. Fowl suggests that Christian claims about the authority of Scripture establish and govern certain networks of relationships. One set of relationships is in regard to its prehistory. A basic Christian claim is that the final form of the Bible is authoritative. "For Christians, then, the Bible is authoritative rather than J, or E, or Q."[25] Also in question is the relationship between the biblical witness to Jesus and the quest of the historical Jesus. The prehistory of Scripture, or its genetics, though not unrelated to the canonical status of Scripture (and of great interest to BT4, for example), is of a different order than the authoritative function it claims by the community in its final form. If there is a distinction between the final form and its prehistory, then there is also a distinction between the canon and any other "text," even one that participates alongside it in the Christian tradition.

While there are a host of texts that help to comprise, articulate, reform, and advance the Christian tradition, they are at the same time entirely expendable in regard to maintaining a Christian identity. This is in contrast to the Bible, which to be Christian one cannot ignore or diverge from.[26] Without wanting to place the cart (church) before the horse (canon), there is an unavoidable meeting-in-the-middle relationship between the Bible's divine status and the community in which it is deemed authoritative and embodied.[27]

Since the scope of biblical theology is rooted in the interdependent two-Testament canon of the Christian church, the sources must then include the full presence of the Christian tradition, with an equally interdependent relation between past and present. Without denying in any way the modern advances in biblical scholarship, BT5 chastises the separation of the text from tradition — that is, the separation of the academy's text from the church's tradition. According to Walter Moberly, "It is common knowledge that the modern biblical criticism only became a recognizable discipline through the process of explicit severing of the classic theological

---

24. For a helpful analysis of the nuances between two proponents of BT4 and BT5 regarding a "Christian" reading of the OT, see Christopher Seitz, "Christological Interpretation of Texts and Trinitarian Claims to Truth: An Engagement with Francis Watson's *Text and Truth*," *SJT* 52 (1999): 209–26; and the response by Watson, "The Old Testament as Christian Scripture," 227–32.

25. Fowl, *Engaging Scripture*, 3. See also Watson, *Text, Church and World*, part 1, especially 30–45, where he offers critical engagement with the application of a "canonical" approach by Childs (BT4).

26. Fowl, *Engaging Scripture*, 4–5.

27. Cf. Wayne Meeks, "A Hermeneutics of Social Embodiment," *HTR* 76 (1989): 176–86.

formulations."[28] Rather than removing historical analyses, the full presence of the Christian tradition embraces such methodologies and lenses in the larger umbrella of the Christian faith—the Rule of Faith. As Watson suggests, this kind of biblical theology "would be a demanding discipline, requiring not only the exegetical expertise traditionally required of biblical scholarship but also the ability to participate with the systematic theologian and Christian ethicist in the contemporary articulation of the Christian faith."[29]

THE HERMENEUTICAL APPROACH OF BIBLICAL THEOLOGY

In its association with the growing interest in a theological interpretation of Scripture, BT5 is concerned to practice theological criticism or theological hermeneutics. A *theological* criticism or hermeneutic is one that is intent on rethinking the relationship between exegesis and theology. While a theological hermeneutic must engage with contemporary hermeneutical discussions, it is unfortunate that much of this discussion takes place in nontheological contexts, where the significance for theology is not self-evident. As can be imagined, there is hardly one approach to a theological hermeneutic. Somewhere near the center of the variety of issues that theological hermeneutics raises, three general approaches can be described.[30]

First, what can be called the "revelationalist" approach is interested in the divine authorship of the Bible, more particularly in the God-world relation "behind" the text. This form of interpretation assumes from the start that a doctrine of God affects the way Scripture is interpreted, while simultaneously acknowledging that our interpretation of the Scripture affects our doctrine of God.[31] The focus is removed away from "what actually happened"

---

28. R. W. L. Moberly, *The Bible, Theology, and Faith: A Study of Abraham and Jesus* (CSCD 5; Cambridge: Cambridge Univ. Press, 2000), 5. According to Christopher R. Seitz, "Scripture Becomes Religion(s): The Theological Crisis of Serious Biblical Interpretation in the Twentieth Century," in *Renewing Biblical Interpretation* (ed. Craig Bartholomew, Colin Green, and Karl Möller; SHS 1; Grand Rapids: Zondervan/Milton Keyes, UK: Paternoster, 2000), 40–65: "The central theological questions receded as the discipline, historically oriented as it has been, simply never ceased to find new historical questions to occupy itself with, and chose to focus on them as though the theological matters would somehow fall into place when all was said and done" (42).

29. Watson, "The Old Testament as Christian Scripture," 231.

30. The following is adapted from Vanhoozer, "Introduction: What is Theological Interpretation of the Bible?" 22–23; and Daniel J. Treier, "Theological Hermeneutics, Contemporary," in *DTIB*, 787–93.

31. See, e.g., Kevin J. Vanhoozer, *First Theology: God, Scripture and Hermeneutics* (Downers Grove, IL: InterVarsity Press, 2002), esp. 15–41.

and placed instead on reading the Bible in terms of divine authorship or "divine discourse."[32] Interpreting Scripture as divine discourse is helpful in discerning the unity among the diversity of the biblical books and for relating the two Testaments. In a similar manner, theological presuppositions about God's involvement and inspiration of Scripture play an important role in how the Bible is interpreted in general, how thematic connections throughout the Bible are construed (i.e., the divinely intended "subject matter"), and how apparent historical inconsistencies are handled.

Second, what can be called the "textualist" approach focuses on the final form of the Bible rather than on questions of human or divine authorship. It is the text in its final literary form that serves as a theological witness. The reader of the Bible participates in the theological witness and discovers God by indwelling the "symbolic world" of the Bible. The concern of this approach is to interpret the Bible emphatically on its own terms, which often means a strongly narrative reading. A theological reading is "intratextual" so that the world of the text, what God was doing in Israel and in Jesus Christ, becomes the framework for understanding the contemporary world.[33] While there are some distinctions in principle, in practice some forms of BT3 (e.g., Richard Hays) could fit comfortably with the textualist approach.

Third, what can be called the "functionalist" approach places the locus of meaning of a theological reading of the Bible in the hands of the contemporary believing community. The reading and reception of the Bible by the Christian community is what gives direction and significance to the theological hermeneutic. The indwelling Holy Spirit, who is best conceived as more active in the present (community) than in the past (event of Scripture), propels the theological reading. What makes biblical interpretation theological is functionally dependent on the aims and interests of the community of readers for whom the Bible is "Scripture."[34]

While these general approaches are not entirely distinct, they clearly approach Scripture with different emphases and have a different outcome in view of a theological hermeneutic. Amidst the diversity there are clear similarities that are worth noting: (1) the intentional shift in social location from the academy to the church; (2) a *critical* inclusivity of the "criticisms"

---

32. See Nicholas Wolterstorff, *Divine Discourse: Philosophical Reflections on the Claim That God Speaks* (Cambridge: Cambridge Univ. Press, 1995).

33. See, e.g., George Lindbeck, *The Nature of Doctrine: Religion and Theology in a Postliberal Age* (Philadelphia: Westminster John Knox, 1984); idem, "Postcritical Canonical Interpretation: Three Modes of Retrieval," in *Theological Exegesis* (ed. Christopher R. Seitz and Kathryn Greene-McCreight; Grand Rapids: Eerdmans, 1999), 26–51.

34. See, e.g., Fowl, *Engaging Scripture*.

of biblical scholarship, especially historical criticism; (3) a focus on the textually mediated message of the Bible; and (4) an interdisciplinary approach that rebukes a hermeneutic that is primarily linear, often deemed to move from Bible (history) to theology, preferring a more holistic, even if ad hoc, approach to the Bible befitting its status as the church's Scripture. Ultimately, therefore, the hermeneutical approach of BT5 involves the formation of a "theological construct" that allows the Bible to function as God's Word for the church.

THE SUBJECT MATTER OF BIBLICAL THEOLOGY

With a clear intent to embrace both the best of biblical scholarship and the robust heritage of the Christian tradition and theology, the subject matter of biblical theology is the collaborative effort of the text's exhortation and the church's embodiment. A pitfall of a biblical theology so centered on a theological hermeneutic is that the complexity of the hermeneutic can turn the method into the end and not the means.[35] And it does feel as if too much ink is wasted on principles of this kind of interpretation and not enough on its practice. Yet for all of its complexity and diversity, BT5 is a return to specifically Christian reading of the Bible *as* Holy Scripture, that is, "authoritative as God's Word for faith and life; thus, to interpret Scripture [is] to encounter God."[36] Such a definition presents a twofold subject matter of biblical theology, one general and one specific.

The *primary* subject matter of BT5 is God and his work in the world. The complex discussion centered on author(s), reader, and text serves to make manifest and witness to the true subject matter: God. But it is not merely God as an abstract idea, but the person and mission of God. BT5 beholds a God who is present and active in the world, a world to which he still speaks through the witness of Scripture. And it is through Scripture that the people of God become participants in the work of God in the world.

Thus, if God is the primary subject matter, the *secondary* subject matter of BT5 is God's people (the church) and their participation in God and his

---

35. The "means" of methodological theory are nicely described by Kevin J. Vanhoozer, "Four Theological Faces of Biblical Interpretation," in *Reading Scripture with the Church*, 141: "Theory describes the necessary features of good practice and explains *why* these features are characteristic of good practice. Theory articulates the regulative ideas (e.g., values, aims, norms) that our interpretive acts and practices always/already embody. It is through these articulations ... that our practices are confirmed, challenged, and corrected."

36. Treier, *Introducing Theological Interpretation of Scripture*, 13.

work in the world. Depending on the classical hermeneutical treatise of the Christian tradition, Augustine's *On Christian Doctrine*, Watson argues that the theological interpreter should be able to attain "a firm grasp of the *telos* of Holy Scripture and its interpretation, which is to engender the love of the Triune God and of the neighbor and nothing else."[37] Fowl even suggests that it is less a hermeneutical theory and more the (corporate) embodiment of Scripture that advances one toward the *telos*.[38] But as Treier helpfully warns:

> For defining this practice there is an even more important word than "church" — namely, "God." ... At its worst, discussion regarding the theological interpretation of Scripture risks criticizing academic biblical studies only to substitute too much focus on the all-too-human activity of the church. But, at its best, the discussion beckons us to view biblical interpretation from the perspective of how — via the past, present, and future activity of Word and Spirit — Scripture teaches the church to know and love God.[39]

In this way God, the true subject matter of biblical theology, becomes both the goal of the church and the grounds for its mission in the world.

CONCLUSION

The fifth type of biblical theology, "Biblical Theology as Theological Construction," seeks a theology of the Bible in overridingly theological terms and based on a theological hermeneutic. The approach of BT5 is a modest critique of the dominance of historical criticism; it serves to incorporate all such criticisms beneath a theological criticism characterized by a governing interest in God and a broad ecclesial concern. Only an explicitly theological biblical theology can make God the primary subject matter and address the issues innate to the church. For too long the academy has usurped the categories of the Bible and its theology and allotted to the church only leftovers. The Bible is the church's book, Christian Scripture, and the theology of the Bible is primarily about God and his work in the world through the church.

---

37. Watson, "Authors, Readers, Hermeneutics," 122.
38. Stephen E. Fowl, "Further Thoughts on Theological Interpretation," in *Reading Scripture with the Church*, 126.
39. Treier, *Introducing Theological Interpretation of Scripture*, 204.

BIBLICAL THEOLOGY AS THEOLOGICAL CONSTRUCTION: FRANCIS WATSON

I t would be hard to find a scholar more connected to the current issues in biblical theology and theological hermeneutics than Professor Francis Watson (b. 1956), formerly reader in Biblical Theology at King's College London (1984 – 1999) and Kirby Laing Chair of New Testament Exegesis at the University of Aberdeen (1999 – 2007), and since September 2007 Chair of Biblical Interpretation at Durham University. While his primary academic field is NT studies, his research encompasses theological hermeneutics and the history of biblical interpretation. Watson's published work tends to move freely between these areas since, as he willingly admits, he is not too concerned about conventional disciplinary boundaries. For this reason the location of BT5 somewhere at the center of theological, ecclesial, and hermeneutical discussions coalesces well with his own research interests and his vision for redefining and practicing biblical theology.

Watson has been involved in a plethora of discussions surrounding theological approaches to a reading of Scripture, but his primary contribution to a proper biblical theology has been established in two ground-breaking monographs. The first monograph, *Text, Church and World* (1994), was an outline for the practice of a "biblical interpretation in theological perspective." Watson develops the following position:

Biblical interpretation should concern itself *primarily with the theological issues* raised by the biblical texts within our contemporary ecclesial, cultural and socio-political contexts ... the familiar but still controversial claim that biblical interpretation should no longer neglect its theological responsibilities is due for a reformulation and restatement.[1]

Such a position demands, as Watson admits, a coordinated effort within both biblical studies and systematic theology. Yet as he also admits, in a discipline dominated by the historical sciences, this is a minority position. Watson reveals in a later work that one reviewer suggested he was "in danger of swapping the exegetes' guild for that of the systematic theologians," which he rightly adds misses "the whole point of the book, which was to challenge precisely this structure of mutually-exclusive, self-contained 'guilds.'"[2] The necessity of this kind of collaboration between disciplines, leading to some kind of constructive coalescence, is central to the approach of BT5.

After reformulating and restating a theological interpretation of the Bible, the second monograph, *Text and Truth* (1997), attempts a "redefining" of biblical theology, as stated in the subtitle (*Redefining Biblical Theology*). No mere rethinking, it is time "to dismantle the barriers that at present separate biblical scholarship from Christian theology."[3] Watson's approach is propelled by a striking conviction: "Modern biblical scholarship has devised a variety of strategies for concealing, evading or denying the simple fact that Christian faith has its own *distinctive* reasons for concern with the Bible."[4] The type of biblical theology Watson envisions contains the best of the offerings from biblical scholarship — including historical criticism, while being contained in the constructive framework of systematic theology, with both serving the interests and tasks of the Christian tradition. In light of the anti-faith posture of most of biblical scholarship, Watson's proposal is robustly constructive — that is, a theological construction. It is to an account of Watson's theological construction for biblical theology that we now turn.

THE BIBLE AS SCRIPTURE: HERMENEUTICS AND DOCTRINE

At the center of biblical theology is the nature and function of the Bible. Watson works hard at proposing a textually mediated theology, which in turn

---

1. Watson, *Text, Church and World*, vii (emphasis added).
2. Watson, *Text and Truth*, vii.
3. Ibid.
4. Ibid., viii.

relies strongly on the nature of the Bible itself. Befitting his concern for an interdisciplinary endeavor, Watson takes great care to explore the integrative task of practicing biblical theology.

For example, Watson is dissatisfied with the either/or approach to a theological interpretation of Scripture: the one solely based on the doctrine of Scripture and the other solely based upon hermeneutical theory. For the former the important thing is what Scripture *is*; for the latter it is what Scripture *does* that really matters. Even more, for the former hermeneutics is perceived to be a threat to the stability and normativity of the Word of God in its written and canonical form; and for the latter the text's divine origin is less significant than its present interaction with a contemporary reader.[5] But Watson suggests that a hermeneutic grounded on a doctrine of Scripture "might make it possible to restate the doctrine of Scripture, or elements of such a doctrine, in a more contemporary theological idiom."[6] More specifically, "conceptuality drawn from general or philosophical hermeneutics can help to address problems of one-sidedness within the doctrine of Scripture or its later development."[7]

But there is more to Scripture than merely the need to be collaborative, according to Watson, for it is the combination of what Scripture *is* and *does* that is most important to the task of biblical theology. Rooted strongly in systematic theology and the Christian tradition, especially the Reformed Confessions of the sixteenth and seventeenth centuries, Watson speaks of the Bible as the Word of God, asserting not just a divine origin but "an identification of Scripture with God's self-revelatory speech."[8] Even more shocking is that the following remark is made by a NT scholar: "To identify Scripture with the Word of God is no mere formality; rather it is to assert the fundamental role of humanly authored texts within the divine economy."[9]

For Watson, then, a faithful interpretation of Scripture must consider the Bible's message as *referring to the present tense*: though grounded in the past,

---

5. Watson considers a representative of the former approach to be John Webster, especially as argued in his *Word and Church: Essays in Christian Dogmatics* (Edinburgh: T&T Clark, 2001), esp. 47–86; and a representative of the latter approach to be A. K. M. Adam, especially as argued in his *Faithful Interpretation: Reading the Bible in a Postmodern World* (Minneapolis: Fortress, 2006), esp. 81–103.

6. Francis Watson, "Hermeneutics and the Doctrine of Scripture: Why They Need Each Other," *IJST* 12 (2010): 118–43 (126).

7. Ibid., 137. Watson helpfully shows the benefit of collaboration between the Reformed Confessions regarding Scripture and the concept of "effective-history" promoted by Hans-Georg Gadamer, *Truth and Method* (trans. Garrett Barden and John Cumming; London: Sheed and Ward, 1955), especially 267–74.

8. Watson, "Hermeneutics and the Doctrine of Scripture," 127.

9. Ibid.

the divine self-communication continues. Contrasting sharply with the traditional values of historical criticism and a large majority of contemporary biblical interpretation, the "Word of God" does not simply occur at the moment of the text's origin (the doctrine of inspiration), but also occurs through the text as "the readers find themselves addressed by God through the scriptural word."[10] For Watson one must be careful to define and interpret the Bible *as* Scripture; only in this way can the "biblical" be truly theological.

THE BIBLE AS HISTORY: THE GOSPELS AS THE NARRATED HISTORY OF JESUS CHRIST

Once the Bible is defined with theological categories, the pressing issue for a NT scholar like Watson is to explore the Bible's overt concern with history, especially in light of two centuries of biblical scholarship in the Gospels, for example, that has been defined almost entirely by historical categories. Again one finds a collaborative effort on the part of Watson, which he expresses through his unhappiness with the attempts of either historical criticism or narrative criticism as applied to the Gospels. Watson argues that "it is possible to combine the orientations toward narrative and toward history by understanding the gospels as narrated history."[11]

This requires, Watson admits, a divergent assumption of historiography and historical research from the assumptions underlying current study of the Gospels. It forces the coalescence between two polar subdisciplines: the one being the narrative-eclipsing tendency of the behind-the-text exploration of historical criticism, the other being the ahistorical tendency of the world-of-the-text storytelling of narrative criticism. For Watson, though correctly portraying the function of narrative emplotment, narrative criticism is ill suited for the real history the Gospels report. Similarly, though correctly exploring the historiographic nature of the Gospels, historical criticism inappropriately demands "that every assertion corresponds precisely to an empirical datum."[12] Rather, by understanding the Gospels to be "narrated history," which "combines the current 'literary' emphasis on the irreducibility of the gospels' narrativity with the conventional 'historical' concern for the relationship between text and reality," Watson offers a more functional interdisciplinary approach that embraces the Gospels' complex nature and witness.[13]

---

10. Ibid.
11. Watson, *Text and Truth*, 33.
12. Ibid., 41.
13. Ibid.

Nowhere is this approach to the Gospels clearer than when he discusses the Historical Jesus project of contemporary scholarship. The thesis for Watson is as follows: "Access to the reality of Jesus is textually mediated."[14] Rooted in what he calls his "theological-hermeneutical thesis," Watson sees a conceptual distinction between the reality of Jesus and its textual mediation.[15] Such a thesis is a modest rebuke of some of the abuses and assumptions of historical criticism, most notably in its claim that to subject the biblical text to a type of questioning it was never intended to answer is an abuse in method. Historical criticism and historical research in general helps to explain and clarify particular features of Jesus' actions and teachings in their context, but these are only "partial clarifications" that are unable to put forward comprehensive solutions.[16] Gathering support from a surprising ally for a NT scholar, Karl Barth, Watson argues for the inseparability of the form *and* content of the biblical texts. Watson quotes from Barth approvingly regarding the history and the books of the Bible:

> With many other things they [the biblical books] do give us something which is recognizable as history, human history in itself as such, but always incidentally, and with all kinds of strange abbreviations and extensions and twists which derive from the fact that *they are really trying to tell us about happenings of quite a different nature*, so that in face of them the historian is always confronted with a painful dilemma: either to let them say what they are trying to say, and not to have any history at all in our sense of the term, or to extract such a history from them at the cost of ignoring and losing what they are really trying to say.[17]

Such an approach is grounded in the Bible as Holy Scripture, which for Watson is best elaborated as the genre of the biblical texts. While a certain amount of historical understanding will assist their function in the social location of the church, not least in giving them an appropriate critical distance, in the grand scheme of things "historical understanding is a very minor component in the more comprehensive understanding that is desirable."[18] By this, then, Jesus is less the historical and more the Jesus of the church — a real, historical Jesus to be sure, but not historical as in "past" but a very present Jesus, a textually mediated Jesus, whom the living Word of God reveals.

---

14. Watson, *Text, Church and World*, 223.
15. Ibid.
16. Ibid., 226.
17. Karl Barth, *Church Dogmatics* (Edinburgh: T&T Clark, 1956–75), IV.1, 505 (emphasis added).
18. Watson, *Text, Church and World*, 228.

Watson's theological hermeneutic is evident not only by his reticence to reconstruct a Jesus from behind the Gospels, but also his concern to receive a four-gospel Jesus. The key question for Christians—who is Jesus?—can only be answered by the fourfold-gospel narration that bears the name Matthew, Mark, Luke, and John. Even more, Jesus is not generically mediated through a text, but through the four Gospels in a tangible way. In a striking statement Watson declares:

> It is the evangelists' Jesus who promises his presence where two or three are gathered in his name; who identifies himself with the hungry and thirsty, with strangers and prisoners; and who gives his own body and blood in the forms of bread and wine. The canonical Gospels are not just a resource for the Christian community, highly valued but in the last resort dispensable or replaceable. On the contrary, they are fundamental to the church's existence.[19]

In short, Jesus is not encountered directly but is mediated through the biblical texts. In light of his definition of Scripture as present-tense revelatory speech of God, such a statement demands that the Gospels play a significant role in the life and worship of the Christian community. No other texts can do; this is why scholarly proposals in regard to the *Gospel of Thomas* or Q are out of bounds for theological (and ecclesiological) reasons: "the outcome would be not only another Jesus but also another community. The community that sees God and the world in relation to Jesus is bound to Matthew, Mark, Luke, and John."[20] With the support of patristic reflection on Scripture and the nature of the gospel, Watson follows Irenaeus (*Against Heresies*), who sees the significance of the fourfold canonical gospel in its testimony to the plurality but also the concreteness of the truth embodied in Jesus:

> Like the living creatures, the gospel is tetramorphon, four-dimensional. Its plural perspectives on Jesus cannot be reduced to one, as though truth were susceptible to a single, definitive account, but neither can they be extended without limit, as though the truth were protean and formless.[21]

Watson also follows Justin (*First Apology; Dialogue with Trypho*), who argues that the four Gospels receive their rationality and coherence by means of their social context in the heavenly liturgy, as described in the book of Rev-

---

19. Watson, "Are There Still Four Gospels: A Study in Theological Hermeneutics," in *Reading Scripture with the Church*, 96.
20. Ibid.
21. Ibid., 114.

elation, and in the ecclesial liturgy as practiced in the early church. "And it is in the Eucharist, itself validated by the canonical Gospels, that guarantees that the coherence of Christian faith is preserved in spite of the plurality of texts. The fourfold gospel has a Eucharistic context and rationale."[22] Rather than presenting a historical case alone, Watson presents a cumulative rationale for a fourfold gospel collection, rooted in the church's own confession and the embodiment of the liturgy displayed in Scripture. Using argumentation that is foreign to modern scholarship on the Gospels, Watson's approach to the Bible and history nearly moves beyond an interdisciplinary approach to something intergalactic—the heavenly liturgy. But such an argument is at home in the Christian tradition and theology, where "empirical data" are made to fit a much more cosmic correspondence.

A CHRISTIAN READING OF THE OLD TESTAMENT: A CHRISTOLOGICAL CONSTRUCTION

Since the beginning of the Christian movement, the OT has always been a problem for interpreters. How can these writings, which began as Jewish Scriptures, be transformed into Christian Scriptures? Watson offers several explanatory theses regarding the "Old Testament" that can be summarized in the following three ways.[23] First, the old/new polarity indicates that "the Christian Bible is irreducibly twofold."[24] It is not enough to speak chronologically; it is essential to understand in regard to the whole of the Bible that each of its parts is part of either the "Old" or the "New." To merge the two parts into a single, linear process is to destroy them both. At the same time, without erasing their distinctions, an understanding must be established between them that allows them to function in a two-Testament relationship. Watson offers an important clarification:

> The Old Testament is old only in relation to the newness of the New; there would be no Old Testament without a New Testament, which can therefore be said to call the Old Testament into being, that is, to constitute an existing collection of writings as Old Testament. Conversely, the New Testament is only new in relation to the Old. Neither collection is self-sufficient; both of them are what they are in relation to the other.[25]

---

22. Ibid., 113.
23. The following is drawn primarily from Watson, *Text and Truth*, esp. the chapter entitled, "Old Testament Theology as a Christian Theological Enterprise" (179–224).
24. Ibid., 179.
25. Ibid., 180.

In this way the two Testaments are both independent and codependent on each other. That is, while they cannot be arbitrarily yoked in a linear fashion, these two independent collections of writings exist in the Christian Scriptures in a mutually constitutive relationship.

Second, the relationship between "Old" and "New" "takes the form of a preceding and a following."[26] What had been the Jewish Scriptures is construed as that which comes before. It contains no center in itself, but merely "points forward to the moment that will retrospectively establish that its reality consists in whatever is implied by 'oldness.'" For Watson the OT does not contain a timeless, unchanging reality in itself, but is entirely contained by the reality that is to come, that is, that to which it points. For this reason the OT cannot be the Jewish Scriptures any longer. In the same way, even the chronological separation of the NT from the OT is not best understood by the measurement of years, for the separation is merely in reference to the appointed time, the moment that definitively established the NT as *the* "New," and the OT as now "Old." Therefore, as much as the OT and NT are related to one another in a chronological manner, it is their qualitative relationship that is most significant. Their relationship is not merely older to newer, for even that which is "Old" is rejuvenated in light of the "New," just as the "New" is made mature in light of the "Old."

Third, as much as there is interdependency between the "Old" and the "New," in light of the arrival of the New and the change in qualitative relations, the New is assigned a certain precedence over the Old. This is not to say that the New supplants the Old, for the relationship must by definition be interdependent. At the same time, however, "in being designated 'old,' the Old Testament is assigned its proper, honored and authoritative place within the Christian canon, precisely as that which prepares the way for the moment that divides the old from the new."[27]

It is only in view of their necessary interrelation that this "certain precedence" can be rightly understood and practiced. While contemporary biblical studies—and biblical theology—has pressured itself to see these two bodies of writings as relatively autonomous collections of texts, such a bifurcation must be rejected by a Christian reading of these texts as part of the two-Testament writings of the Christian tradition. That is, while historically a separation is sensible and likely even mandated, theologically even the hint of separation is already out of bounds. Such a distinction separates BT5 from

---

26. Ibid.
27. Ibid.

BT2, for example, which views the relationship between the Testaments as running along the developmental-historical redemptive purposes of God, or from BT3, which views the connection primarily through intertextual linkage.

For Watson, the contemporary misunderstanding of an autonomous OT is rooted in the abstraction of these texts from the sole context in which they can be meaningful for Christians: the person and work of Christ. The primary context of the OT is not Ancient Near Eastern history or even the continuing history of communal usage (Jewish); rather, the primary context is in relation to Jesus himself. "From the standpoint of Christian faith, it must be said that the Old Testament comes to us *with* Jesus and *from* Jesus, and can never be understood in abstraction from him."[28]

Watson admits that this is a theological judgment, one rooted in the qualitative relationship between the two Testaments, which find their meaning and even source in Jesus. Thus, according to Watson the Christian church receives the OT with Jesus and from Jesus. It is received "with" Jesus because he is the *meaning* of the Scriptures, since from his arrival even the OT Scriptures were never understood to be referring primarily to anything other than testimony to Jesus. And it is received "from" Jesus because he is also the *source* of the Scriptures; since his resurrection Jesus sent his apostles to proclaim to all nations the good news about God's definitive act for the salvation of humankind.

This approach to the OT is exactly how the first Christians responded, both Jewish and Gentile, and is reflective of a Christian and theological approach. Unlike modern scholarship, there is no unease about the Christian context and roots of the OT. The OT is not a natural or neutral entity; rather, it is an essential part of the two-Testament Christian Scriptures.[29]

Watson defines this understanding of the whole Bible and the motivation for his theological hermeneutic as a "christological construction." "Christian faith requires a *christocentric* reading of Christian scripture ... for in Jesus Christ the identity of God, the creator who is also the God of Israel, is definitively disclosed in the triune name of Father, Son and Holy Spirit, for the salvation of humankind."[30] This forms, for Watson, a "theological framework which is often more implicit than explicit" within which detailed exegesis occurs.[31] The person and work of Christ also become a "Christ" concept that can serve to unify a range of biblical material that might otherwise have been disparate and unimportant.

---

28. Ibid., 182 (emphasis added).
29. Ibid., 182–83.
30. Ibid., 185.
31. Ibid., 320–21.

This christological construction is part of a theological hermeneutic that "has learned to see the scriptural texts in the light of Christ, and Christ in the light of the scriptural texts."[32] Similar to the theologically defined nature of Christian Scripture, this hermeneutic is founded on the creative theological judgments and imagination commonly used by systematic theology and the history of the Christian tradition.[33]

GIVING REDEFINITION TO BIBLICAL THEOLOGY: CONSTRUCTING A THEOLOGICAL HERMENEUTIC

Francis Watson's contribution to biblical theology has been centered on a biblical interpretation that is theological in perspective. It is not a precise method; rather, it is an approach to the Bible that takes primarily into account the theological issues raised by the biblical texts within our contemporary ecclesial, cultural, and socio-political contexts. Rather than a method, its only creed is that "biblical interpretation should no longer neglect its theological responsibilities."[34] As Watson says in a more recent book on Paul and hermeneutics:

> What I hope to show is that an open-ended theological orientation is integral to any exegesis that engages seriously with the text and its subject matter. This theological orientation does not need to draw attention to itself as such, for issues of contemporary theological concern are bound to come to light whenever the scriptural texts are read with empathy and insight.[35]

Thus, for Watson, a "redefined" biblical theology is open-ended in its theological orientation and is sensitive to theological "issues" and theological "concerns" within the contemporary context. It is, in short, a reformulation and restatement of the innate theological nature of Scripture.

While Watson is reticent to offer a pure "theological" method, he does willingly speak of a theological "framework." For Watson biblical interpretation occurs within what he describes as three concentric circles: text, church, and world. The "text," as we described above, is the Christian Scripture, which must be read and interpreted in a manner befitting its unique nature

---

32. Ibid., 325.
33. Although Watson's approach resembles the christological approach of the "Philadelphia school" of BT2, there is still a noticeable distinction between them. Although Jesus is central to the hermeneutic for "Philadelphia," history still remains the overarching structure. Jesus is still mediated by means of the historical development of redemptive history.
34. Watson, *Text, Church and World*, vii.
35. Francis Watson, *Paul and the Hermeneutics of Faith* (London; T&T Clark, 2004), x.

and purpose. The "church" is the primary reading community, within which the biblical text is located. The church is the *audience* to whom Scripture is addressed and is the worshiping *context* into which its proclamation is to be heard and responded to. "If theology is to be Christian ... the ecclesial community must be seen as its primary point of reference."[36]

At the same time, Scripture is not an enclosed message but one that extends to the "world," which in its ecclesial sense refers to the vast social space that surrounds and encompasses the church, within which the church is to fulfill its mission. Without denying the church as the primarily social location for interpreting Scripture, the world does offer a possible source for truth. Even more, just as Scripture must be embodied in the church, so also must the church be embodied in the world. The church makes public claims in the world, a Christian proclamation regarding truth and reality, for ultimately the biblical story is also the story about the world. For Watson, then, "there seems to be no reason in principle why biblical interpretation should not be practiced within this hermeneutical framework."[37] It is a particular theological construction that intersects text, church, and world in a biblical-theological framework for interpreting the Word of God and participating in the mission of God.

It is with all of this in mind that Watson claims that "this interdisciplinary interpretive practice may be appropriately named *biblical theology*."[38] Such a definition is concerned to maintain the appropriation of the "biblical" and the "theological." Even more, Watson desires to keep the title without succumbing to the errors so common to the practice of biblical theology (e.g., the Biblical Theology Movement). Yet to do so will require some redefinition of the title, for the biblical theology he is advocating must be redefined within a specific theological and hermeneutical situation. A "redefined" biblical theology must be able to answer the criticisms leveled against biblical theology so that they will not be repeated, and at the same time to move the practice of biblical theology forward in order to fulfill the calling of the contemporary church in the modern/postmodern world.[39]

ASSESSMENT

For Watson, biblical theology is ultimately a theological hermeneutic performed in a theological context (the church) with predominately theological

---

36. Watson, *Text, Church and World*, 6.
37. Ibid., 11.
38. Watson, *Text and Truth*, 8.
39. Ibid., 8–9.

categories (a theological construction). Although Watson applies historical-critical methods to the text of Scripture, he is hesitant to let historical criticism dominate the reading strategy. Rather than making biblical interpretation primarily a historical exercise, Watson is unhesitant in his desire to bring all the interests of systematic theology into his biblical theology. In a similar manner Watson makes explicit his concern that the Bible be read as Christian Scripture and in a Christian context, in contrast to the academy, which has become the standard social location for the Bible and its interpretation. While Watson's robust redefinition of biblical theology is commendable, a few concerns can briefly be addressed.

If by itself Watson's interdisciplinary approach were not complex and controversial enough, the relationship of his biblical theology to the growing movement of the theological interpretation of Scripture only muddies further the water of his definitions and methodological approach. Clearly he is involved in both camps (systematic theology and biblical theology), as well as being a NT scholar (a third camp that in its contemporary form has a strong aversion to anything theological). For this reason Watson is hard to place, since he moves seemingly effortlessly between three quite different domains—and this is to exclude the domain of the church, which figures so prominently in his hermeneutic.

Thus, the difficulty in understanding the specifics of Watson's approach to biblical theology is parallel to the complex debate in general regarding the more recent interest in all things theological, for which he has become a frequent spokesperson.[40] Even beyond the difficulty of defining his bold embracing of theological categories and methods, such a position is surely to face the onslaught of attacks by the majority of scholars who almost exclusively adopt historical-critical assumptions and reading strategies. Thus, Watson is not only swimming around in very muddy water, but he is also swimming upstream.

Even among friends, however, Watson's approach to biblical theology has not gone without criticism. At the more general level Stephen Fowl has argued that Watson's "theological interpretation" is not theological enough. After noting that Watson uses terms like "theology" and "theological" in relation to the distinct discipline of systematic theology, Fowl argues that systematic theology has "been subject to the same anti-theological disciplinary forces of the modern university as biblical studies has been."[41] Fowl stands

---

40. Watson frequently appears in the survey of the theological interpretation movement by Treier, *Introducing Theological Interpretation of Scripture*, 19, 64–68, 117.

41. Fowl, *Engaging Scripture*, 23.

with others who protest against the academy's version of systematic theology for being dominated by modern, academic categories.[42] According to John Milbank, the university-based systematic theology has been dominated by models dependent on the social sciences and modernist philosophy:

> The pathos of modern theology is its false humility. For theology, this must be a fatal disease, because once theology surrenders its claim to be a meta-discourse, it cannot any longer articulate the word of God, but is bound to turn into the oracular voice of some finite idol, such as historical scholarship, humanist psychology or transcendent philosophy.[43]

Scriptural interpretation is a practice that can only shape and be shaped by specifically Christian convictions and practices, rooted in the unadulterated community that embraces a common life. Thus, for Fowl, Watson is not theological or ecclesial enough.

A more specific challenge has been offered by Christopher Seitz in regard to Watson's christocentric hermeneutic. According to Seitz, Watson's proposed solution to the necessary two-Testament Bible forces a choice between the OT and NT by placing a "but" and not an "and" between Jesus of the NT and the God who is known through his self-disclosures to Israel of the OT.[44] Seitz argues that Watson's christological interpretation not only mutes the "discrete voice" of the OT, but it also distorts the relations between the two Testaments and the God being witnessed to: the trinitarian God. For Seitz only a trinitarian reading of Scripture is large enough to embrace the full identity of God and the diverse manifestation of God's self-disclosure in the Old and New Testaments. Seitz's conclusion is worth quoting in full:

> The discrete voice of the Old Testament is not something even sympathetically "Jewish" which must be carefully handled if the linkages to Jesus Christ are to be properly displayed and celebrated. The Old Testament is not a relative with a gas problem, as a former colleague once said, that we must accept and try politely to work around. The Old Testament is the witness of the One God with whom we have to do, who has sent his Son for the salvation of the world, breaking down a dividing wall and bringing those who are far off near by the blood of Jesus Christ. The Old Testament has a horizon that is

---

42. Fowl relies specifically on the arguments of John Milbank, *Theology and Social Theory* (Oxford: Blackwell, 1990), esp. chs. 5, 8, and 12. Cf. Christopher Rowland, "An Open Letter to Francis Watson on *Text, Church and World*," *SJT* 48 (1995): 507–17.

43. Milbank, *Theology and Social Theory*, 1.

44. Seitz, "Christological Interpretation of Texts and Trinitarian Claims to Truth," 220. See also a similar and more robust critique of Watson peppered throughout Christopher R. Seitz, *The Character of Christian Scripture: The Significance of a Two-Testament Bible* (STI; Grand Rapids: Baker, 2011).

not exhausted in what we can say about Jesus, for its language and its divine promises lie not behind the New, but show the way ahead of the New that fulfillment may be a promise made good on, to the glory of the Father, who with the Son and Holy Spirit is One God, unto the ages of ages.[45]

Thus, for Seitz, christological interpretation "warrants our attention only to the degree to which it conforms with trinitarian truth about God, and conveys exegetical and interpretive guidelines commensurate with that truth."[46]

The concerns voiced by Fowl and Seitz, who can claim to be "plowing the same field," reveal the complexity of a theological approach to the Scripture.[47] Watson's theological hermeneutic has rightly been described as eclectic and iconoclastic and having been influenced by another controversial figure: Karl Barth.[48] As much as Watson has helped move the discussion of a robustly and unashamedly biblical theology and theological hermeneutic forward, because of the complexity of a theological approach he has also inadvertently added more clutter in the path.

---

45. Seitz, "Christological Interpretation of Texts and Trinitarian Claims to Truth," 226.
46. Ibid. In response to Seitz, Watson, "The Old Testament as Christian Scripture," implies that Seitz's "Trinitarian" preference merely covers the separation that still exists between the two Testaments, which for Watson cannot be allowed: "To speak of the 'discrete witness' of the Old and the New Testaments respectively is to make an important point about the twofoldness, but it tells us nothing about the dialectical unity" (227). Thus, what is needed is a Christian rereading of Scripture that can "enter more fully into their living dynamic" (230).
47. Fowl, *Engaging Scripture*, 22.
48. See Treier, *Introducing Theological Interpretation of Scripture*, 19.

CONCLUSION: UNDERSTANDING BIBLICAL THEOLOGY

Defining biblical theology is notoriously difficult. Even agreeing on the particular set of issues that ought to be raised in a biblical-theological study is controversial. Without a clear consensus regarding what biblical theology is and how to do biblical theology, we have merely attempted to set out a taxonomy of ways biblical theology is currently practiced.

Our desire is that plotting each of these types with representative practitioners along the continuum between history and theology will offer a degree of substance and clarity concerning the elusive idea of "biblical theology." As we noted in the introduction, this is only a heuristic schema, a lens through which readers might perceive and visually organize the panorama of theological reading of the Bible. Though bearing the title *Understanding Biblical Theology*, this book is not an answer to the problem of defining "biblical theology." Rather, it is an attempt to draw attention to some of the central issues attending the task of biblical theology along with a practical consideration of some of the more visible thinkers working in the area. We offer no new definition or methodological proposal for biblical theology because we envisioned our task as clarifying the morass of definitions and proposals plaguing both the academy and the church.

We would be the first to admit that this book was difficult to write. In order for the book to be helpful and functional, it was necessary for us to explain these five types of biblical theology with brevity, knowing full well that each type could receive a book-length treatment on its own. In fact, we hope that future works on biblical theology will be benefited by our taxonomy and avoid talking past each other, a practice that has in recent years become something that seems to have been copyrighted by practitioners of biblical theology. We are also aware that the five scholars we presented as examples of the types were treated with a selectivity that has the potential to pigeon-hole their position and perspective or minimize their truly remarkable contribution to the field at large. Our intentions were much more pure.

It is also important to make clear that we were well aware that each type of biblical theology is not best defined narrowly. Rather, each type reflects a diversity of definition and expression that might also be viewed as containing within it a continuum. Several types express this diversity. BT2, for example, contains such a clear continuum of diversity that we were able to use geographic reference points representing the institutional sources of nuanced trajectories within that type. The debates of the last generation regarding the interpretation of the OT and eschatology between John Walvoord ("Dallas school") and George Ladd ("Chicago school") have not only solidified positions, but have served to prove that the positions were similar enough that tension between them would naturally take place. This is all the more evident in BT3 in the more recent, public disagreement between N. T. Wright and Richard B. Hays. The fact that they cannot simply talk past one another is a reflection of their relatedness.

In an attempt to guide readers as they survey these types of biblical theology, we offer a summary of how each type addresses the central issues we surfaced in the introduction. At every turn we have attempted to give order where, at times, there is chaos. Yet, even with our best attempt at organization and clarity, we fear that readers may still fall into a crevasse never to be seen again! We offer this guide in hopes not to lose any readers — even more, to help make key, summative comparisons between our five types of biblical theology (see chart on pp. 186—89).

CONCLUDING REFLECTION

The idea for this book grew out of both our fascination and frustration with biblical theology. Our fascination was over *how* the Bible renders the coherent story of redemption — how the Bible, a historical document, renders theology. Our frustration surfaced as we began to encounter the vast jumble of attempts at reading the Bible theologically — how "the theology of the Bible" is very much a disputed statement. Rather than offering a definitive account of the state of biblical theology or, even less, a full-scale attempt to define biblical theology, the aims of this book are much more discrete. In the end we hope to initiate a dialogue that might both clarify the notion of biblical theology and encourage its practice in the life of both the academy and the church.

From its inception this book has been looking beyond itself, to the discussions that will (and need to) take place in regard to biblical theology long after this book has played its part—as a simple map to get the discussion moving in the right direction. But we would be remiss if we did not end with an eye toward the continued discussion of the theories and practices of biblical theology. Two forecasts are worth hoping for and reflecting upon.

First, we hope this book will help explain *why* the academy finds it so hard to make sense of the differing versions of "biblical" in biblical theology. The longer that biblical theologies and biblical theologians speak past one another, the more quickly the term "biblical theology" will become a nose of wax, so pliant it loses any sense of its own boundaries or form. While we have offered proof that biblical theology is pliant, at least according to the five types we described, such descriptions also serve as proof that biblical theology does have its own boundaries and innate form. The academy needs to work hard to retrieve the substance of biblical theology, even if debate is allowed to remain in regard to the exact nature and outworking of that substance.

Second, we hope this book will help explain *how* the church has been and should continue to express their "theology" by means of biblical theology. If the academy (i.e., universities and especially seminaries) is speaking past itself in reference to its definitions of biblical theology, the result is a further deepening of institutional distinctions and isolation between research trajectories. But for the church the result is devastating. Institutional distinctions and isolated research trajectories might facilitate the individuality and ingenuity of a professor's standing in the academic guild, but a debilitated biblical theology is entirely crippling to the mission of a pastor and the vision for the people of God.

The questions plaguing the contemporary discussion of biblical theology are central to the life of the church, such as, for example, the nature and relation of the two-Testament Christian Scripture. For the church biblical theology is not a method or a field of study; it is a way of life. And if for no other reason, we hope that this book will facilitate pastoral discussion of the role of biblical theology in and for the church, and maybe more simply, how pastors—and not just professors—can actually practice and contribute to biblical theology.

SUMMARY OF TYPES

	OT relation to NT	Historical Diversity vs. Theological Unity
BT1: Historical Description	There is no proper relation between the OT and NT. By historical standards they are separate documents, which necessitates that they be handled by different academic disciplines and, sometimes, separate religious traditions. There is no warrant for forging a relationship between them.	The category of history disallows an externally applied theological unity. By not forcing unity, the individuality of each of the documents (e.g., Matthew and Luke) and of even the two Testaments serves to highlight their diversity and "natural" irrelation.
BT2: History of Redemption	The OT and NT relate by means of the employment of a "special history," that is, redemptive history. After the individual redemptive acts of God on behalf of humanity have been aligned chronologically, the Testaments are then unified by thematic-typology (e.g., kingdom, covenant). Unity can only be secured by exegetically derived thematic-typological connections that allow for the networking of two different, historical entities.	The category of a "special history" allows for a theological unity that is defined with precise thematic-typological links that are primarily historical in nature. This special history, however, only allows for a general unity that must also demand a large amount of historical diversity. Even in their unity the Testaments are noted for their individuality, and corpora and books are especially recognized for their unique contribution.
BT3: Worldview-Story	The OT and NT relate by means of the larger narrative or story of Scripture. From the outset the unity of the two Testaments is assumed, with the category of narrative serving as the lens through which their relation is defined and understood. Where a "narrative unity" cannot be established, a "narrative substructure" of the non-story genres is established to connect the Bible from Genesis to Revelation.	The literary category of "narrative" and the philosophical category of "worldview" serve to unify the parts of the Bible into one grand story, with controlling emphasis given to the narrative genre. Within the confines of story, the historical diversity is perceived as related acts of the unfolding biblical drama. The reality of Jesus Christ sheds light on and integrates the history of Israel into a story that connects ancient Israel to the contemporary church.

OF BIBLICAL THEOLOGY:

Scope and Sources	Subject Matter	Church vs. Academy
Because the subject matter is the historical event "behind the text," any source that aids in its access, from inside or outside the canon, is gladly welcomed. It is not the Bible itself (i.e., the canon) but the social and historical contexts that determine the scope and sources of BT. Priority is given to any source that best describes the actual, historical people, places, and events.	The subject matter is determined by the historical situation of the documents themselves. It is what the Bible meant "back then" in the past. The original, historical, cultural event "behind the text" is the desired goal. Because the subject matter is entirely historical, the method of choice is historical criticism.	BT is under the ownership of the academy. No ecclesial or theological presuppositions are allowed (as in BT4 and BT5), only the "neutral" discipline of historical investigation. BT is not concerned with the contemporary Bible; systematic theology is required to interpret and translate the results of BT for the church.
Because the "special history" involves real history, the use of extrabiblical sources is warranted, even demanded. As a bridge between exegesis and systematic theology, BT is rooted in the real, historical contexts of the biblical texts. The canon, however, serves as a filtering guide, limiting the force and use of extrabiblical sources to matters pertinent to the specific nuance of this theologically constructed history of God's actions.	The subject matter is the "special history" of God, frequently including Jesus Christ at its center. It encompasses the progressive history of God's actions across both Testaments. This subject matter requires a historical-exegetical method that allows for theological movements and connections (e.g., (kingdom, covenant) given warrant by the category of "special history."	BT is constructed in the academy, but is quite frequently used in and for the church, especially in preaching. Since BT is a functional "bridge discipline" between exegesis and systematic theology, it is one of the primary tools of the pastoral ministry. It assists the church as it tries to understand God's ancient message for modern life, often done by comparing "special history" with contemporary history. The inductive nature of BT2 results in numerous practical, topical studies based on key themes derived from the Bible.
The scope of BT is rooted in the canonical story line of the biblical narrative. There is often a strong reliance on extracanonical sources in order to "read" or construct the story assumed within the context of the historical narratives. The sources may include whatever resources are necessary to interpret the metanarrative of Scripture, which also often includes the dramatic worldview assumed outside the canon as theatrical backdrop for the biblical narrative.	The subject matter is not the historical or social context "behind the text" (BT1) but the interconnected story line running "through" the text. The subject matter is derived categorically from both story, the explicit narrative to be read, and philosophical construct, the implied worldview of the authors/readers. The method requires one to read the stories "behind" and "in" the text for the purpose of proclaiming the story "in front of" the text.	BT is constructed and maintained directly between the academy's narrative tools and the church's living script that is already being enacted and lived out. The union is better in theory than in practice, however. For some the academy is the primary constructing agent, for others the church's contemporary story and practice. Ultimately both are required to play their part.

	OT relation to NT	Historical Diversity vs. Theological Unity
BT4: Canonical Approach	The OT and NT are related as a unified witness without losing their discrete voices. Their relation goes beyond historical sequence by moving the discourse to the ontological plane. The two Testaments find their relation in the dynamic relationship between the historical-critical study of the Bible (e.g., tradents, redactional activity) and its theological use as religious literature. The historical diversity yields a unified theological witness to its true subject matter: Jesus Christ, who is the divine reality underlying the entire two-Testament canon.	The category of canon alone is able to handle the grand diversity of the historical documents (and their progressive editing) alongside the theological unity to which they cumulatively testify. Only by embracing both historical diversity and theological unity can the full, symphonic message be heard and appropriately passed on to the contemporary church.
BT5: Theological Construction	Since its reception within the Christian community, Scripture must be defined as both Old and New Testaments. Their relation is not only chronological but also qualitative: the Old matures the New, and the New rejuvenates the Old. But while there is mutual give and take in the relationship, precedence is given to the NT, for through the fullness of the NT Christ is encountered, who is the key to understanding the OT. It is not the interaction with the subject matter that unites the Testaments (BT4), but the subject matter itself that establishes their unity.	By beginning with the category of Christian theology, which is ultimately both theological and ecclesial, any semblance of historical diversity is either contained or omitted. The Bible is by definition an in-house document—not an ancient text but the church's Scripture. As such, approaches that view historical diversity by means of categories foreign or uncontrolled by Christian theology are disregarded. Scripture contains a theological unity because it is given ontological emphasis as the unified Word of God, in contrast to diversified human words.

Scope and Sources	Subject Matter	Church vs. Academy
The scope and sources of BT are drawn from both the Bible's historical locations and its ecclesial location. Set within the framework and guidance of the community of faith, all the historical-critical tools of the academy are utilized. These tools probe not the event "behind the text," but the textual tradition within the canon, the intra-canonical tradition (canonical prehistory and editorial reinterpretation), requiring numerous tools traditionally used for historical construction.	The subject matter begins with a description of the biblical witnesses to their ultimate object toward which they point: Jesus Christ. This is in sharp contrast to a subject matter determined "behind the text" (BT1). The method for this subject matter moves from witness to subject matter by an exegetical procedure that pays careful attention to the canon's original witness and context, but also the text's subsequent reinterpretation in new contexts.	BT is ultimately a property of the church, even though the tools of the academy are necessary. The hostility between them can be tempered by means of their ordered and functional partnership. The academy explores the textual traditions that have been received, collected, transmitted, and shaped through different times, cultures, and languages; the church functions as the applied audience (past and present) for whom the texts serve as their life, identity, and obedience. But the church is ultimately the supportive framework, since the canon is foundationally a confessional category.
The scope and sources of BT are derived from the theological context of Christian Scripture. What is determinative is the theological nature of the Bible, with the church as its primary social location, and Christian theology as its primary frame of reference. While the scope is limited to the final form of Scripture, the sources are increased to include the history of Christian tradition. Sources concerned with the Bible's "background" (BT1 and BT2) are expendable, but "foreground" sources, like the "Rule of Faith" and creeds, demarcate the boundaries for Christian theology and BT.	The subject matter is primarily God and his redemptive work in the world. Not God as an abstract idea, but God, made known in Jesus Christ, who is actively engaged in his creation, speaking through Scripture to redeem a people for himself and making them participants in his work. The secondary subject matter is God's people, the church, and their participation in God's redemptive work. The method for this subject matter is rooted in what Christian theology deems to be the goal of Scripture and its interpretation: love of God and neighbor.	BT is under the ownership of the church. The proper context for BT is in the worshiping community; in this setting, the dogmatic presuppositions of Christians are given primary priority over the so-called "neutral" presuppositions of historians. The critical methods of the academy are critiqued and controlled by means of Christian theology. From its inception BT is engaged as a discipline paying immediate normative dividends within the believing community. Only in the church can the Bible be handled by its true form and nature.

SUBJECT INDEX:

AUTHOR INDEX

Share Your Thoughts

With the Author: Your comments will be forwarded to the author when you send them to *zauthor@zondervan.com*.

With Zondervan: Submit your review of this book by writing to *zreview@zondervan.com*.

Free Online Resources at
www.zondervan.com

Zondervan AuthorTracker: Be notified whenever your favorite authors publish new books, go on tour, or post an update about what's happening in their lives at www.zondervan.com/authortracker.

Daily Bible Verses and Devotions: Enrich your life with daily Bible verses or devotions that help you start every morning focused on God. Visit www.zondervan.com/newsletters.

Free Email Publications: Sign up for newsletters on Christian living, academic resources, church ministry, fiction, children's resources, and more. Visit www.zondervan.com/newsletters.

Zondervan Bible Search: Find and compare Bible passages in a variety of translations at www.zondervanbiblesearch.com.

Other Benefits: Register to receive online benefits like coupons and special offers, or to participate in research.

ZONDERVAN.com/
AUTHORTRACKER
follow your favorite authors